The Last Authority

Three Decades of Nigeria's Contribution to the Liberation Struggle in South Africa

By

Oboshi Agyeno

The Last Authority: Three Decades of Nigeria's Contribution to the Liberation Struggle in South Africa

By Oboshi Agyeno

This book first published 2023

Ethics International Press Ltd, UK

British Library Cataloguing in Publication Data

A catalogue record for this book is available from the British Library

Copyright © 2023 by Oboshi Agyeno

All rights for this book reserved. No part of this book may be reproduced, stored in a retrieval system, or transmitted, in any form or by any means, electronic, mechanical photocopying, recording or otherwise, without the prior permission of the copyright owner.

Print Book ISBN: 978-1-80441-131-5

eBook ISBN: 978-1-80441-132-2

DEDICATION

To my mother and the Motherland.

CONTENTS

Acknowledgement vii

Foreword ix

PART 1: INTRODUCTION

Introduction 3

PART 2: COLONIALISM BY ANOTHER NAME

Apartheid in South Africa 35

South Africa, a Nation in Distress 51

Africa; Call to Action 59

Africa has come of age 77

Frontline States plus Nigeria 87

Multilateral and Back-Channel Diplomacy 95

Fellowship of Brotherhood 107

PART 4: GREEN LAND AND DISTANT RAINBOW

Consider all Options for Freedom in South Africa 115

There is no National Interest 120

Resentment in Post-Apartheid South Africa 131

PART 5: AFRICA, KNOW THYSELF 143

Reverse Ubuntu 145

The African Renaissance 151

Nigeria-South Africa Day 158

Bibliography 167

Index 169

Acknowledgement

I am grateful to God Almighty for the opportunity to see and take this book from conception to completion. I am immensely grateful to many brilliant personalities whose insights and comments shaped the content of this book. In a very special way, I want to acknowledge and thank H.E, Prof. Ibrahim Gambari, H.E, Dr. Tunji Olagunju, H.E, Dr Dele Cole, H.E, Dr. Martin Uhomoibhi, and H.E, Ambassador John Ejinaka. These experienced diplomats had, on different times, shared their views on the subject matter and opened my eyes to several perspectives. I sincerely thank them for affording me the time to sit with them and chat. I sincerely thank Ms Boshigo Matlou, a South African who lived, schooled and worked in Nigeria during the apartheid era. I truly appreciate your discernment and consultations.

My gratitude also goes to Prof. Andreas Velthuizen of the Thabo Mbeki School of Public and International Affairs, University of South Africa for giving me the chance for a postdoctoral fellowship. I appreciate the good working relationship cultivated with the entire staff of the former Institute for Dispute Resolution in Africa (IDRA) now the Thabo Mbeki African School of Public and International Affairs, University of South Africa. I also thank the staff of the Institute for Peace and Conflict Resolution (IPCR), Abuja who have one way or another, contributed in making this book a reality.

While I also thank my family for their support and push for this book to come to fruition, I will specifically thank my Twin, Abari, for painstakingly and diligently working on the format and design of the book. A special gratitude also goes to Mr Naanlep Raymond for the encouragement and unrelenting support. I also thank Mr Olaniyi Abodedele, publisher of the Nigerian Voice Newspaper in South Africa for the consultation, and your insight enriched this book. I appreciate the contribution of Mr. Philibus Musa Dangrem, a friend indeed. A huge thank you also goes to a cerebral personality, my friend and brother, the award winning writer and functionary of the Association of Nigerian Authors, Mr. Omale Allen Abdul-Jabbar for a good work done in editing and proofreading the work. Let me also thank the Editor in Chief, Biographical Legacy and Research Foundation (BLERF), for painstakingly working on the book index. This book is a reality because of you all. *ASANTE.*

Foreword

History records the events of the past relating to particular places or subjects, preserved as a guide for the future. History ensures that the legacy of the past is secured as part of the inheritance of future generation. It is therefore empirically important that while recording such history, deliberate steps should be taken to ensure the inclusion of the most infinite details that enables the inquisitive mind to have a better knowledge of the event, how it happened and who played major roles therein, the various *dramatis personae* that are worthy of mention and preserved for posterity.

The Apartheid regime in South Africa, remained one of the ugly pasts of colonialism in Africa and one whose history must be fully detailed without any form of dilution as Africa was united in the fight for freedom for South Africa. The oppressive administration of the white supremacist regime in South Africa became more vicious at a time when most of Africa had gained independence. It was therefore little wonder that the rest of Africa having attained political freedom almost at the same time, were collective in the quest to join forces to ensure that the remaining vestiges of colonialism in Africa was totally eliminated.

The Sharpeville massacre of March 1960 provided African leaders with the needed impetus for collective action against the evil of Apartheid regime in South Africa. Reacting to the Sharpeville massacre, the Nigerian Prime Minister at the time Alhaji Tafawa Balewa, in 1961, just at the threshold of Nigeria`s independence wrote to the leadership of the African National Congress, extending a hand of support, a position subsequent Nigerian leaders sustained until the final liquidation of Apartheid. In the case of Nigeria, the initiative by the various Nigerian government widened the scope of engagement to include participation and contribution of every Nigerian both in cash and kind towards the liberation struggle in South Africa. The Nigerian government went the additional mile to provide hundreds of Nigerian international passports to many members of South African freedom fighters whose passports had been confiscated by the leadership of South Africa who now had to travel under Nigerian passport in their quest for freedom for their country. Many South African students were given scholarship which enabled hundreds of South African students to continue their education in Nigerian higher institutions.

Unfortunately, the post-apartheid history of South Africa had avoided the leading role played by some African countries, in particular Nigeria in the liberation struggle. Nigeria was so involved in the liberation struggle and the impact of its support so profound that there is no single African country that would claim to provide the kind of influence that Nigeria brought to bear in the liberation struggle. Nigeria's role in the anti-apartheid movement was so great that it earned Nigeria the membership of the Frontline States, an appellation used to describe a coalition of countries in southern Africa that shared proximity with South Africa, but most importantly countries whose government and people dedicated their sovereignty, resources and emotions to fight the white minority regimes propelling apartheid in South Africa. Nigeria was considered a Frontline state and a great ally of the oppressed people of South Africa in appreciation of her leadership role and near physical presence in most decisions of the Frontline States in the fight against apartheid.

It is this missing link, and inappropriate documentation of the role of Nigeria in the struggle to defeat apartheid that prompted Dr. Agyeno to embark on this project. He has therefore taken all the necessary steps, to provide some of the details on the contribution by Nigeria and some other countries, in particular the frontline states towards the liberation of South Africa from Apartheid regime. He shared the view that if the Nigerian role and those of other African states were properly documented, it would have gone a long way to correct the mind set of many South African youths, many of them born after the death of Apartheid and who had failed to acknowledge that they were not alone in the struggle but that other African leaders worked tirelessly towards the emancipation of South Africa. The effort by Nigeria, saw to the expulsion of Apartheid South Africa from the Commonwealth in 1961. It also underscored the consequences for Nigeria when she took some bold steps towards the nationalization of some of the tangible assets of the British government in Nigeria, to the dismay of many from the west. That step by Nigeria signified to the global community Nigeria's readiness to take every measure necessary towards dismantling apartheid and to do whatever it takes to win freedom for South Africa. Dr. Agyeno further posited that were the South African youths better educated, they would have extended a hand of friendship to Africans who came to South African after the collapse of Apartheid instead of the resultant xenophobia that greeted the Africans as well as Nigerian migrants to that country. The young South Africans saw the African migrant as a threat to their newly acquired freedom and therefore the unfriendly attitude towards them even when the African migrants are legitimate residents and with verifiable means of livelihood. The action of the South African Youths and the deliberate neglect from the South African elite was contrary to the Pan African spirit that pioneered the liberation struggle, and worked for their liberation, the spirit every South African should be expected to cherish.

The role of diplomacy in the liberation struggle was not left out, as the book underscored the role of Nigerian diplomacy at all levels in the collective fight for the liberation of South Africa. Nigerian diplomats in major capitals of the world lobbied and solicited support from their host governments to join in the struggle and to give support for the South African course.

Dr. Agyeno took time to provide information about the economic capabilities of South Africa which at the time was the economic power house of Southern Africa, a position it still occupies till date. The location of South Africa made it possible that major neighboring states are dependent on South Africa for its access to the sea, a position it exploited effectively in its relations with those states while the apartheid system lasted.

It is a book every lover of history would like to have.

Ambassador John Chika Ejinaka

PART 1: INTRODUCTION

CABINET OFFICE,
LAGOS,
NIGERIA.

Ref: PPS.27   4th April, 1961.

Sir,

    Alhaji Sir Abubakar Tafawa Balewa, Prime Minister, has directed me to thank you for your kind letter of the 19th of March and to assure you that on his part, the battle against apartheid has just begun.

        I am, Sir,

           Your obedient servant,

           (A. Ahmed Kari)
       Ag. Principal Private Secretary
         to the Prime Minister.

Mr. M. Herbstein,
P. O. Box 238,
Abeokuta.

A letter confirming Nigeria's commitment to end apartheid immediately after independence

Introduction

History, despite its wrenching pain cannot be unlived, but if faced with courage, need not be live again.

Maya Angelou

"Khawuleza mama, hurry mama don't let them catch you"

Miriam Makeba 1961

On a cool November spring in South Africa, an annual conference was underway in one of the most prestigious Universities where papers on xenophobia, black on black violence and other regional conflicts are being discussed. The African hall, which was incidentally the venue where six papers were presented by predominantly foreign scholars and students was full to capacity. The paper presentations on that particular day would have just been as the day before it, but on this day, there were more disturbing perspectives on the presentations around xenophobia. The conversation veered towards that period of the liberation struggle, when the African brotherhood was prominent against apartheid and indeed when Africans got each other's back. While the discussion was still being reflected on the subject matter and the debate generating the needed attention from the audience, there was a jaw dropping silence among the foreign participants at the African Hall when a guy who I would later come to identify as Dlamini, blurted out in the middle of the argument that 'nobody helped us during apartheid, and with a spat he went further to ask on top of his voice;

'where were other Africans during our darkest moment'? Dlamini was outwardly referring to his own understanding of how he thought black South Africans were deserted by other African countries during apartheid. He gave the impression that majority black South Africans were abandoned by fellow Africans during apartheid. The response of Dlamini elicited a thunderous applause across the hall.

As expected, some voices in the hall grew louder and I couldn't help but notice that these voices were coming from Nigerians and other foreign participants who were trying to concur to the narrative of African solidarity during the anti-apartheid movement. That didn't make any difference because the session became rowdy as the young South African students that made half of the population in the hall kept applauding Dlamini as he spoke so eloquently, raising his voice above any other, about what he thought he knew of the liberation struggle and how apartheid in South Africa was fought and won. In my startled concentration, I heard him say that it was only Julius Nyerere of Tanzania that offered them land to cultivate and a place to stay when many of them had to go on exile during their period of oppression, humiliation, desolation and isolation that became the hallmark of the majority in apartheid South Africa.

No doubt, majority of native South Africans were isolated during the apartheid regime, but not isolated by other African countries. Since Dlamini mentioned Julius Nyerere of Tanzania as the only African in his memory that supported native South Africans during the liberation struggle, I quickly interjected and asked him if he knew the place of Samora Machel of Mozambique, Kenneth Kaunda of Zambia, General Murtala Muhammed of Nigeria, and Seretse

Khama of Botswana in the schema of the liberation struggle?. He was about to answer the question with a smirk of assurance on his face when the program director and time keeper insisted the session was over.

During tea-break, I saw Dlamini sitting at a table sipping coffee while talking on his cell-phone. I cautiously made my way to where he was enjoying some snacks and asked if I could share the table with him. He says if you want, with a hand gesture to suggest I take a seat! Now anyone could notice that Dlamini was popular with the audience and participants at the conference. I would later understand that he is a known activist and a local champion of post-apartheid South Africa. As I sat beside him, I went straight to question why he thought that only Julius Nyerere gave respite to native South Africans during apartheid.

He answered with a more relaxed tone, leaning backwards to rest his back on the chair's splat. Of-course there were leaders like Kwame Nkrumah and Muammar Gaddafi he said, who were there for the oppressed people of South Africa. I nodded in acceptance of the two leaders he mentioned while still asking him if he knew the contribution of Nigeria to the liberation struggle. I got a shiver at his response. Dlamini insisted that Nigeria did nothing for South Africans and if any, it was the late General Sani Abacha of Nigeria who was planning to send weapons to the freedom fighters to engage in armed conflict against apartheid shortly before he was 'killed', and that plan never materialized. According to Dlamini, the 'gift' from Sani Abacha of Nigeria would have given the freedom fighters an edge in the liberation struggle had he not suddenly died.

I tried to explain to him that there were several African actors in the liberation struggle of South Africa that changed the course of the anti-apartheid movement to the advantage of the oppressed majority of South Africa, but he seemed to care less. The conversation got me perplexed, and more surprising was that the ignorance displayed by Dlamini was shared across a large number of native South Africans, especially those referred to as the 'born free'. The born free are a generation of large youth population of South Africans who were born around the end of apartheid or when democracy and majority rule was ushered into South African political space. The born free are young, curious and gullible, they make up about 40% of South Africa population. They are among the students that filled up the African hall when the arguments of whether other Africans supported the natives during the anti-apartheid movement or not. The born free are very impressionable.

Anyway, my inquisitiveness got me asking a broad spectrum of the South African demography of their impression of the role of Nigeria during apartheid. So many do not know what Nigeria did and very few acknowledged the contributions of Nigeria. You could see that those who knew about Nigeria's contribution during the liberation struggle were the population that left South Africa on exile during apartheid, who unfortunately do not see it as their responsibility to tell the youngsters stories of Nigerian comradeship or even document the assistance or value they got from Nigeria or other Africans when on exile to those countries. Besides, these set of South Africans were noticeably few and quite elderly.

Nevertheless, after acknowledging superior arguments from some scholars who came to join our conversation, Dlamini unapologetically conceded that some help did come from African countries during apartheid and apart from the Julius Nyerere angle, whom he said gave them land to live and cultivate for food as exiles in Tanzania, Dlamini also added that Kwame Nkrumah of Ghana and Muammar Gaddafi of Libya should be applauded because these personalities also gave support in cash and kind to the liberation struggle. He made this statement with the confidence of a typical South African involved in activism. What then could have happened to the history of notable individuals and countries who stood against apartheid, and yet are not even political or religious leaders but ordinary citizens spread across Africa who gave enormous material and psychological support to the liberation struggle?

Those class of people or country didn't bother Dlamini. I decided to further stir the conversation around the contributions of Nigeria to the liberation struggle from a different angle to test his sense of history. I asked Dlamini if he knew about Chief Emeka Anyaoku of Nigeria who contributed significantly in enthroning democracy in South Africa, and who incidentally holds a national award in South Africa of 'the status of a Supreme companion of OR Tambo (Gold)'; which is South Africa's highest honour for a non-South African? He responded that he would have known if there was any significant support from any such Nigerians in that regard. He went on to say that, 'the ANC can decide to honour whoever they please, and it does not reflect the wishes of the people'. He did not know who Chief Emeka Anyakou is, and does not pretend to care whatsoever.

The highest honour bestowed on Chief Emeka Anyaoku was given to him during the presidency of former president Thabo Mbeki. Chief Emeka Anyaoku was the Secretary General of the

Commonwealth of Nations and worked assiduously during that period to dismantle the blocks of apartheid in South Africa and ensure a peaceful transition to democracy and majority rule. Regardless of the positioned he held with the Commonwealth, he was before then a foreign affairs minister in Nigeria for a brief period of time, and has mediated individually and through official capacity, to resolve the crisis between the ANC and the Inkatha Freedom party of Mangosuthu Buthelezi, which ignited internal conflicts and violence among factions of the two parties and their supporters. This led to killing of Africans by Africans and that was seen as a dent on the spirit of the anti-apartheid movement. The crisis undermined the liberation struggle from the African perspective and thanks to the interventions of people like Chief Emeka Anyaoku, it was resolved and some normalcy and purpose returned that will eventually usher South Africa into democracy.

Well, many 'born free' South Africans do not know about the history of the liberation struggle. Shortly after the conference, I was gripped by a sense of guilt not because Dlamini's outburst jolted me to the reality that Africans know very little about Africa, but that knowing very little about African history by Africans themselves has influenced the kind of peculiar challenges in the relationship that the continent is currently contending with. From insecurity, underdevelopment, distorted coexistence and irresponsible leadership. The system that was built after democracy and majority government was enthroned in South Africa, downplayed the place of history in the education of its future generations. This is prevalent in the life of the native South African. These South Africans are not aware of some historical truth that have shaped their present configuration as a country, nor do they care to understand the historical significance of Pan Africanism displayed on their behalf by African countries in the past.

Yet, Pan Africanism is evidently acknowledged among native South Africa as a means to an end, an end that could showcase the good in our Africanism, from the colour of the skin to the originality of thoughts, deeds, aspirations and relationships. The lack of emphasis on South Africa and many other African countries in teaching history in schools and other institutions of knowledge and learning has disturbingly increased in proportion. It is also responsible for the indignities of self-hate persona and inability to manage diversity ascribed to Africans in domestic and international politics. Little knowledge on the positive impact of past exchanges within the continent and inability to use such knowledge to build a modern, united and interconnected societies by Africans themselves is arguably the original sin of the black race.

In fairness to the first generation of political leaders in South Africa which consist of Nelson Mandela and Thabo Mbeki, subsequent political leadership of South Africa disregarded important historical facts that should be embedded in the heroic narrative of African resistance to oppression and colonialism in modern democratic South Africa. Perhaps, the multifaceted challenges that confronted these leaders in building a modern and inclusive society, distracted them from exploiting the value of African comradeship already laid down by previous leadership to construct a knowledge driven society that draws strength from the past to build a cohesive future.

Many people in South Africa do not have an idea that Nigeria was a core member of the liberation struggle and instrumental to a lot of persuasion that ended apartheid. To this end, I had to do something, anything but stay silent over a rich historical element on African solidarity, brotherhood and unity of purpose displayed during the liberation struggle. The liberation struggle was a period when Nigeria projected the Africanist paradigm of its foreign policy, which was expressed meaningfully in South Africa during the anti-apartheid movement. But deliberately or by default, that part of history of African solidarity and resistance was and is still being ignored by those who benefited the most from the Africanist posture of Nigerian foreign policy first hand, and those who should know better what Nigeria contributed during such period. Some accounts of such contributions are documented and others acknowledged by not only the first generation leaders of South Africa, but by other African leaders and historians. Even the simplest oral tradition of storytelling in Africa could have passed down and communicated this aspect of Africa's rich and impressive history of resistance to the young and increasing population of the people of South Africa. Alas, that part of history is silent in South Africa.

There have been several accounts of assistance that some African countries deployed to end apartheid in South Africa, as there is no denying the role Nigeria played. How come then that the contribution of Nigeria is obviously absent in the narrative of anti-apartheid movement in South Africa? That aspect of history of Nigeria contributions against apartheid in South Africa is muted across the length and breadth of the country, on the streets, by its government, people and the national sentiment of South Africa. It is strange that the lacuna created by the ignorance of African solidarity and resistance by native South Africans themselves, have invariably made South Africans to think that other Africans living in South

Africa are sabotaging the South African interest. Over time, this situation has made Africans to live perpetually in fear and anxiety of discriminatory and intolerant behavior by South Africans, instead of having a sense of camaraderie which should have normally been ignited by the history of friendship cultivated by past African citizens which gave a sense of purpose, brotherhood and *Ubuntu*.

It is the impression of this author that if African history is told by those who lived it and those who knew how African ancestors cooperated and intermingled with each other in the past, then perception of Africans will change about themselves in more accepting ways, and the intolerance they have for diversity and contradictions will begin to diminish. Individually or collectively, it should be known for a fact that African countries deployed enormous resources to support the people of South Africa against apartheid. The attempt to be silent on such solidarity and supports in itself is a recipe for grievances and lack of accommodation for each other.

So in my disappointment and disbelief with the level of ignorance on the role played by some African countries particularly Nigeria during the liberation struggle, I set out to interview the people of South Africa from Pretoria to Limpopo, the Free State to Kwazulu Natal. The born free' generation and a large number of the elderly to my astonishment weren't acquainted with the contributions of other African countries in what appeared to be the last political struggle for the dignity of the black race in Africa by Africans. Many in South Africa do not have knowledge on how the liberation struggle was won. To them, the intermittent revolts, strikes and civil disobedience against the draconian rule of apartheid carried out by the natives living within South Africa itself was the silver bullet. Little did they know that some of these strikes, boycotts and demonstrations were planned and executed from outside of South Africa, with the support of the 'friends of freedom'

As far as most South Africans know or think, those who fought bravely inside South Africa did it alone and successfully without help from anywhere but by the good fortunes of the ancestors. Even some of the elderly who were young during such period were either reluctant to admit knowledge of assistance that the oppressed people of South Africa received from outside of South Africa, or were plainly also ignorant of it. After some deep reflection, the idea to excuse such ignorance became acceptable because the period when the dark cloud of ruthless oppression, discrimination and servitude hung directly over majority of South Africans, the country was pretty much closed out from the rest of the world. This could be the reason why many native South Africans aren't aware of the contributions of Nigeria or other 'friends of freedom' against apartheid South Africa. There could be other reasons to this ignorance, some of which shall be interrogated as we move along. However, the seeming ignorance of the contributions of African countries in ending apartheid became the inspiration for this book.

The 'Last Authority' captured as the title of this book is figurative and deliberate for many reasons. First, South Africa was the last country in Africa to gain political freedom or what others will prefer to call independence from erstwhile colonial administration in the continent. Put succinctly by Olayiwola Abegunrin (2009) in describing the history of colonialism in Africa, 'the white settler regime in South Africa was the last white rule regime to surrender power to an African majority government in the continent'. Secondly by its location, South Africa is the last country located at the bottom tip of the African continent where land meets marine. Indian oceans to the east and the Atlantic Ocean to the west.

Lastly, the three decades in focus by this book reflects the last era that Nigeria successfully flexed its political, economic and diplomatic muscle and implanted the Africanist agenda on the international arena to restore, prevent or dissuade the indignity of the African person. Whether it is to end apartheid or salvage war torn countries from civil wars and annihilation, Nigeria in the 1970s, 1980s and 1990s was the last period that many remembered in deeds and words of how truly powerful and manifest Nigeria was in Africa. The chapters put forward will highlight some of the contributions made by Nigeria to the people of South Africa against white minority rule, a regime that was to be the last political stronghold of European incursion in Africa. This is a historical narrative of the liberation struggle in South Africa from the paint, brush and canvas of Nigeria.

＊

The Republic of South Africa is a sovereign state and many of its ardent citizens aligned with the black consciousness movement of Steve Biko will prefer to call Azania. Without argument however, South Africa is fondly nicknamed 'Mzansi" by majority of its young population and indeed the natives. Mzansi is a slang word used by the aboriginal people which connotation means 'the South'. It is by every description a very unique country in Africa with a climate like no other and certainly the most industrialized yet. South Africa is the last country at the tip of the southern-most part of the continent of Africa where the expanse of its land is located between the Atlantic oceans to the west and Indian oceans to the east. The only country in Africa blessed to have the vastness of its land surrounded and touched by these two great oceans.

It is also the last country in Africa to gain political independence by the majority to decide and determine their future from white minority administration in 1994. Indeed, the process of attaining freedom or independence of majority South Africans did not come cheap. Those who sacrificed everything to accomplish majority rule and democracy for self-actualization of the natives in Mzansi did it at a great cost, many paid the supreme price for such freedom. As would be expected in such instances by the oppressed people of Mzansi, very deliberate efforts have been put in place to immortalize those who risked everything to make sure that true democracy, majority rule and freedom to the people was achieved.

The names of Pixley ka Isaka Seme (founder of what is now known as the African National Congress) Albert Lithuli, Oliver R Tambo, Govan Mbeki, the famous Nelson Mandela, Thabo Mbeki, Solomon Mahlangu, Stephen Bantu Biko, Robert Sobukwe, Chris Hani, Tebeho Mashinini, etc. have all played heroic roles in deliberately fighting for freedom of their people in different ways, time, space and season. The struggle for such freedom by these personalities and others demanding for self-determination from the white minority administration in Pretoria at the time, revealed one of the most horrific, oppressive, inhuman and sinister system of subjugation ever recorded in recent memory within the continent of Africa. It also revealed one of the most remarkable and perhaps the last of the stories of purposeful leadership by Africans to liberate Africa, and of African resistance and solidarity against foreign political oppression, and promoting the dignity of the black race.

Apart from the very gallant and sustained effort to liberate the people of *Mzansi* from the evil system of apartheid by South Africans themselves, the collaboration and contributions of other sister African countries in particular, and the international community in general, was significant if not pivotal in overthrowing the apartheid regime in South Africa and indeed the Southern Africa region as a whole. The exploits of African countries in the anti-apartheid movement have been often told by foreigners or from the position of an outsider looking in, instead of the other way around.

Apartheid was a sinister arrangement of official discrimination, illegitimate domination and denial of rights to majority of South Africans which by implication offended the sensibility and civility of the black race. It was a constitutionally racial oppression that was heaped on the black majority of South Africa and which was introduced by the National Party in 1948. 'Apartheid denied the most basic democratic and human rights to some 87 percent of the population. The majority of South Africans have been barred from the right to vote, to own land, to live outside specially designated "Bantustan" and urban 'group areas', or to hold certain industrial and other jobs reserved for whites' (Steven Clark,1993:9).

During the entire period apartheid lasted, the aboriginal people along with other people of colour residing in South Africa were forced and obligated to live in a cluster which the apartheid regimes called the homeland or Bantustan. This homeland was to be a separate country made up of habitation of squalor within South Africa and which will belong to the natives, while the white minority confiscated and occupied all the rich agricultural land and shared it among themselves. The native majority lived in cluster of shanties and forced to inhabit a sparsely allocation that constitute only thirteen percent of South African's land. In contrast, the whites lived, farm and controlled a vast expanse of land that is two times the size of Netherlands. The whole idea about the Bantustan was to remove the blacks from the urban areas, and remove the right to self-determination from the natives, and push them out of sight so they don't mix with white communities, except with permission. The Population Registration Act in 1950, the Bantu Homelands Citizenship Act of 1970 among others therefore, sealed the implementation of this policy of segregation. (www.sahistory.org.za)

The impact of the policy of segregation in South Africa through several Acts by the National Party was to simply deprive and remove the choices, power and identity of the native majority by enacting different laws under apartheid that will strip the natives of their place to access any political rights, factor of production, and even the right to keep their language. The Soweto uprising in 1976 that witnessed the barbaric killings of school children who were demonstrating the substitution of their mother tongue in schools with Afrikaans as the medium of instructions was another milestone in the gamut of apartheid policies in South Africa which the natives vehemently resisted.

The natives of South Africa had put up a strong resistance to apartheid and its draconian policies across the country. There was no other way to resist these policies than to fight for their inalienable rights with uncommon perseverance and insist that human rights has a universal application. It was thus inhumane to deprive a black man or woman the right to vote or reside anywhere they deem fit, but allow the minority unfettered access to vote and be voted for. It was on this moral breadth that the fight for liberation kept occurring either through careful planning or sporadically. Fortunately, many African countries who were opposed to these injustices had shown solidarity in contributing to the success of such resistance.

The contributions of some notable African countries gave the impetus for the blacks in South Africa, who were naturally in majority to record the series of successes that gave the liberation struggle a pass mark and an example of an African led civil resistance against colonialism on a global scale. During this period, African countries displayed a strong sense of solidarity and shared interest with the oppressed people of South Africa. The quest for freedom in South Africa became a collective responsibility and interest which manifested in the support the native majority of South Africans received from regional and national governments and people of Africa.

Unfortunately, over many decades of enjoying the fraternity and monumental support from Africans to end apartheid in South Africa, inadequate knowledge and information are available to South Africans themselves on the extent of assistance and contributions they receive during the liberation struggle. This is particularly true about the contributions of African countries in fighting for the freedom of South Africa and the confrontation with the white minority government in Pretoria during such period.

Young South Africans on whose shoulders is the future of *Mzansi* are not aware of how the liberation struggle was executed and won through the support provided by other African countries.

Among the friends of freedom are African countries like Nigeria that played an influential role in closing the chapter of apartheid in the continent. The ignorance displayed by young people across the length and breadth of South Africa and the perceived silence by the government of South Africa who are incidentally the biggest beneficiaries of the liberation struggle, will not change the fact that the liberation struggle was a fight to liberate the people of Mzansi, of which several African countries contributed their quota. There is no denying the fact that South Africa and its people enjoyed the benevolence and spirit of Ubuntu from other Africans before, during and shortly after apartheid was eradicated.

Ubuntu for a black man or woman, is an idea that many have argued originated from Africa or have captured the essence of African civilization more than any other. It is the thinking that explains the nature and substance of African political, social, economic, environmental, spiritual and communal understanding of life. Ubuntu is fixated on the concept of humanity and yet more concern with how this human being thrive, relate and perceive other humans in his or her community.

Ubuntu is therefore a tale of African humanism and the projection of the African character. In Mandela's wisdom, he opined that 'Ubuntu is a profound sense that we are human only through the humanity of others; that if we are to accomplish anything in this world, it will in equal measure be due to works and achievement of others'. The above statement with the benefit of hindsight suggest that Africa can only make rapid and remarkable progress when Africans work together. It indeed shows the interconnectivity of human life for so long and in varied ways that the concept of Ubuntu from the African perspective over the years have come to bear a global viewpoint or application.

Ubuntu can therefore be applied to governance, entertainment, science and technology, law and every angle of human circumstance and conditions. This is what gives Africans a group identity and it does not matter the location, belief, ethnicity and religion of a person, Ubuntu aligns the hope, expectations, aspirations and development of the black race into one sturdy and unified agenda. Ubuntu is the African version of being your brother's keeper, a translation that speaks of the significance of communal responsibility that escorts a black man or woman, where ever he or she may be. This is deeply rooted in African orientation and could be interpreted in several ways, yet speak of the same thing.

It is on this basis that Nigeria in particular and other African countries did not look away when their kin in South Africa were under the evil machination of apartheid. Nigeria, united with other African countries confronted apartheid with all they got. Yet many years later, the history of such unity and solidarity in resistance to foreign domination and oppression was silenced, misconstrued, cleverly removed, diluted or out rightly denied. It is expedient to document the information of such solidarity for South Africans and every global citizen to know and learn from it. The silence in African collaboration, solidarity and unity among Africans themselves will later have its consequences across the continent, in which the manifestations of some of consequences are particularly seen in South Africa.

Information about the role played by several countries in the continent of Africa during the liberation struggle need to be recognized through storytelling at least, and at best, through folklore and songs, which are Africa's basic logic of communication. These stories should be widely acknowledged in forming the camaraderie needed in African unity. This is necessary for the simple reason of aligning the past to the future, so that the native majority of South Africans will know that some countries if not the entire continent of Africa was with them during their darkest moments. This is important to consider as a subtle way in improving relations among Africans living in South Africa in particular, and black solidarity across the world.

It is also necessary to change the mindset of people like Dlamini on what he thought he knew about the history of the liberation movement. After all, the older generation of South African leaders like Nelson Mandela and Thabo Mbeki have acknowledged the contributions of Nigeria to the liberation struggles at different occasions in the past (Nigerian Voice Newspaper 3013). However, statements of Nigerian contributions to the liberation struggles are made in isolation and not to the crowd that should appreciate such effort. There is a strong level of ignorance among South Africans who often hold true that they were betrayed by other Africans when they needed help during apartheid. Even the involvement of the frontline states (FLS) in ending apartheid is only spoken passively.

This text intends to reveal some essential historical details of the liberation struggles from the Nigerian perspective that was left out or not spoken about, whether deliberately or by default in South Africa. Stories inside South Africa recount countries like Libya, Egypt, Ethiopia, Tanzania, Ghana, Angola and Zambia as the regular contributors to the liberation struggle in South Africa. This could only be half of the story. There was a time that the contributions of Nigeria which came immediately after her independence was extensively acknowledged, and such contribution from Nigeria had raised the standard and impetus that the liberation struggle came to be so regarded.

For instance, even though the focus of this book is limited to the contributions of Nigeria to the liberation struggles from the 1970s, it is instructive to note that Nigeria started fighting against apartheid at the very moment it gained independence and became a sovereign member of the international community. In 1961 when Nigeria became a member of the International Labour Organization (ILO), Nigeria moved the proposal of expelling apartheid South Africa from the organization. This call was resisted by western nations who said the ILO should not be mixed with politics. After three years of Nigerian insistence and dogged persuasion however, the Nigerian position prevailed and South Africa was suspended from the ILO.

Curiously enough, the blame for such level of ignorance and obliviousness by many young South Africans who do not know about the history of the liberation struggle and contributions of notable countries like Nigeria that occupied a pivotal locus in eradicating apartheid may have come from a deliberate policy of silence by the African National Congress (ANC) members, government and the South African media. The media in post-apartheid South Africa adopted the same strategy that the white minority government used during apartheid to delete some facts from the history of the natives. This situation according to David Letsoalo (2022) 'is a desperate attempt to depoliticize and de-historicize the act of resistance (sic) and it's our responsibility as black people in this country to wage the fight against distortions and defacement of our rich historical truth'. The South African media after 1994 was dominated by white chauvinist and their cohorts, so it is palpable to understand why they omitted, water down and ignore some historical accounts of the support of African countries, especially the account of Nigeria towards apartheid and the liberation struggle.

This is apart from the neo-liberal argument in some quarters that dominated global thinking during and after the cold war, to which dislocated learning in building African indigenous knowledge. Historical facts have always been illuminating the direction of relationship in Africa and some forces who do not want the rich African history to be transformed for public good, are doing everything to make Africans forget or be shamed by such history. Subsequently, the continent became disenchanted from its own knowledge generation as there was a short supply of historical information that is necessary to guide future generation and learning.

Anyway, the ANC was the biggest beneficiary of the liberation struggle and have been in power since democracy and majority rule was instituted in 1994. It is the opinion of this book that the ANC deliberately handpicked the countries in Africa that they choose to celebrate as positive contributors to the liberation struggle and muted the contributions of Nigeria to the struggle for reasons best known to it. There may be some historical assumptions for such silence by the ANC, and that will *be* discussed.

The relationship between successive Nigerian governments and the ANC during the liberation struggle fluctuated based on exigencies between 1970s up until democracy and majority rule was established in 1994. For instance, the apparent support and recognition that Nigeria gave to other organizations in the struggle like the Pan African Congress (PAC) and other groups as equal partners to the ANC during the liberation struggle could have greatly irritated the ANC. Besides, Nigeria at some point did not fully understand or trust the ideological standing of the ANC, which was socialist inclined and radical. This leaning have made some government regimes in Nigeria uncomfortable or wary of any likely revolt that it may influence within the Nigerian populace. Regardless of this, every Nigerian government has made individual commitment in extensive measure to the anti-apartheid movement.

In fairness to all the voices calling for freedom within and outside South Africa during apartheid, Nigeria tried to accommodate the various opinions, strategies, methods and expectations that had been generated. In a liberation movement such as this, it is common for comrades to disagree on some approach to goals and objectives. The non-racial consideration of the rights of equality to everyone living in South Africa as a basis for negotiations was not a consensus. There were those who wanted an armed struggle to seize power from the white minority or they be made to hand over power and asked to leave South Africa. But to end apartheid, the rights of every human being living in the country had to be recognized first, as there were a considerable interests of other races who also vehemently oppose the apartheid system with great sacrifices.

Nigeria and other friends of freedom eager to end apartheid saw that a non-racial South Africa was the most plausible demand and expectation at that material time. Some factions and disagreement were noted but at the end, a multi-racial equality got the best offer. However, that has angered some group that make up the freedom fighters in South Africa who would later show disdain for Nigeria or refuse to acknowledge the special role Nigeria played in the struggle, despite some of these people being the biggest recipients of such arrangement.

For a long period in the history of the struggle, the ANC saw itself as the sole representative and officialdom in the driving seat of the liberation struggle and do not wish to share such accolade, responsibility and visibility with any other organization, especially not any organization that was perceived to be a breakaway from it. That was how the ANC viewed the PAC, South African Communist Party (SACP) and other of such organizations like the Black Consciousness Movement. However, from the Sharpeville massacre to the Soweto uprising, several players emerged that directly or indirectly removed the attention of the liberation struggle away from a single denominator. Strong characters emerged that will challenge the authority of the ANC and in consequence, create different agendas to end the oppression and segregation that was apartheid. Nigeria was gracious to all parties involved in the struggle, so long as the freedom is achieved. This aspect did not settle nicely with the ANC and which will later make the ANC snub

Nigeria even in public pronouncements as 'comrade in arms' of the struggle.

Another argument for the silence may have come from an ideological perspective as noted earlier. Nigeria's disposition to capitalist free market economy did not appear as an example of a country that should get compliments for the liberation struggle since it will contradict the philosophy of the struggle. Nigeria during apartheid was a capitalist-oriented entity and it is still that. But the ideology that gave impetus and legitimacy to the liberation struggle rested on communist dictum. At that time, all the mass of the oppressed South Africans were psyched up by communist (or socialist if you like) gyration and it would have seemed an anomaly for Nigeria that had no ideological bases on an egalitarian society to be able to fill their heads with hope of a proletariat revolution, or the overthrow of the few by the majority. This was one of the reasons why Kwame Nkurmah of Ghana and Julius Nyerere of Tanzania had more acceptance with some South Africans when talking about the liberation struggle than perhaps Tafawa Balewa of Nigeria. It was the ideological connections they had with the liberation struggle that mattered most to the people of *Mzansi*.

Kwame Nkurmah and Julius Nyerere spoke to the deep yearning of freedom that was burning in the hearts of native South Africans. It was easy for South Africans to therefore remember these personalities and acknowledge their countries more in solidarity than any other within the continent. When the freedom of a nation is taken away, the voices of people that resonates in the deep of those in captivity may last longer than any material exploit to freedom. Thus, it seems that the call for the unity, emancipation, liberty and

Africanization of the continent by Nkrumah and Mwalimu Julius Nyerere made a lasting impression on the people of South Africa than the millions of dollars, military, strategic and covert assets that Nigeria deployed to end the apartheid system. Nigeria did not bother to insist or see apartheid as an ideological trap, instead a racial and ethnic character of domination orchestrated by foreign element inside the core of the black race.

So, just like any system of oppression that apartheid in South Africa came to represent to the people, ideological resistance to it played an important role. Ideology makes more meaning to a people who feel lost and in need of a mental direction or encouragement. This makes the intangible impact more than just material support. To the wise, when freedom is taken away, the appreciation of material benefit takes a back seat. However, it is by far a display of witlessness to think that the material support for the liberation struggle is any less than the idea itself.

Kwame Nkurmah insisted that we must find an 'African solutions to our problems, and that this can only be found in African unity. Divided we are weak; united, Africa could become one of the greatest forces for good in the world'. The charisma, power of oratory and the sheer brilliance of Kwame Nkrumah was a source of inspiration to Africans seeking true emancipation of the African person. This endeared Kwame Nkrumah as one of the voices to reckon with in understanding and inspiring the idea, philosophy and impetus of the liberation struggle in South Africa. Every African should thank Nkrumah for such inspiration.

But the contributions of political goodwill, material and financial assistance by Nigeria made tremendous impact to the liberation struggle and this could not be undermined because in the final analysis, the Nigerian foreign policy was African centered, and the people of Nigeria in that period were favorably disposed to revolutionary thinking and the Africanization of political independence in Africa. This was done by the government and people of Nigeria while expecting no reward in return and questioning the rationale of national interest. According to Joe Garba (2012), it will be fallacious to believe that we (Nigeria) can base our national interest, and to wit, foreign policy on anything other than a quid pro quo. After all, apartheid was also a political economy intention as yet a racial contemplation. This may have been supported by Pierre du Toit when he argued that in South Africa, the debate has tended to focus primarily on the relationship between capitalism and apartheid and to a lesser extent on related subjects such as the Afrikaner nationalism and the class/racial/ethnic character of the anti-apartheid movement.

Some particular set of observers have also argued that Nigeria by its attachment to capitalism and western dogma could not have given any significant support to ending apartheid because it may indirectly be benefiting from it. However, such argument has failed to realize that what Nigeria saw in apartheid was not necessarily a political system that contradict socialism or communism, but also a racial contrivance. The moral position of Nigeria to end white minority government in South Africa was beyond politics or capitalist creed, but a firm articulation to defend the dignity of the black race in their motherland against foreign invasion. As far as Nigeria was concerned, the liberation struggle was a fight for freedom, the restoration of dignity of the black race and eradication of any form of colonialism from the African continent. By its content and purpose, Nigeria's support for the liberation struggle and the role it played was largely successful and should be acknowledged.

***

Today, your first impression of South Africa when you arrive at any of their major entry points, will be largely of an infrastructure manifestation barely seen anywhere in the continent. Its people, diverse, cosmopolitan and brave in many respects, are fun loving and endearing. It would be a complete volume on its own to talk of the scenic beauty of this illustrious country and a compelling climate hardly seen anywhere else in the continent. *Mzansi* is certainly a darling of all who live in it and a land of promise with enormous potential to redirect Africa into a progression of power as the last frontier of development. But the history of South Africa and of its native people have been enmeshed in degrading experience for so long that anyone who visits *Mzansi* for the first time, would think that the natives of South Africa have lived plush all their lives.

Not so long ago, all of native South Africans have faced oppression, discrimination, repression, injustice and persecution at the behest of a white minority government. The sovereignty of the natives which is intricately linked to their land as the main factor of production and source of wealth, power and foundation of life, was taken away from them in a brazen manner by non-Africans. This followed a series of deprivation that will strip the natives of their dignity, riches and humanity.

When asked to give a profile of how post-apartheid South Africa would look like at the end of apartheid, Joe Garba, one of the forerunner in driving Nigeria's policy of the liberation struggle asserted that 'decades of apartheid have left a painful legacy of distrust and anguish and this persist despite the resilience and courage of those who wish to see their country on an irreversible new course'. He went further to buttress that 'the violence factor and of course, the obvious inclination of radical whites to resist any attempts at changes that will deny, whittle away, or undermine those privileges they enjoy under apartheid, will continue to pose the most difficult problem in post-apartheid South Africa'. This prediction appears to be valid in current experiences of Mzansi. As much as there is democracy and opportunities appear to be accessible to more of the native majority, yet the white minority still determine those opportunities and the scale of such access. The liberation struggle still persists in a different dimension.

However, the criminal and inhuman conditions unleashed on the natives of Mzansi by Europeans for many years inevitably put these benign group of people at a quandary of self-hate and disdain for foreigners. It was made worst that even after democracy and majority rule was achieved, the natives have been located at the bottom of the country's economic and social ladder, (just as Joe Garba opined earlier), and their freedom was still determined by a subtle apartheid contraption. Most distressing for them is that the hangover of apartheid has left the natives bitter and in many ways intolerant to others they perceive as different or foreign. This condition is manifesting itself in many dimensions, exposing racial tension resonating in elusive statecraft, prejudice, insecurity and incongruity. The eclectic consequence of apartheid on the natives is a major foray in understanding community transformation in contemporary subjects of reconciliation, nationalism, colonialism and imperialism, immigration and diversity.

The young black South Africans are conscious of the historical facts that situate them in the harsh condition that they face in their country. However, such condition could have been handled differently in a manner that extol strength in diversity if they knew the support they got for democracy to come to them, and if the government had told them of the African solidarity that helped to achieve it. In the knowledge of such solidarity exemplified in the liberation struggle, maybe there could be a better negotiation to the challenges of political, social and economic challenges that confronts development in modern South Africa. These young natives do not know the full story from the African context on how they came to be referred to as the 'born free' generation. But how could you even blame this generation of Africa's future, when the entire continent is progressively saddled in dwindling oral tradition of knowledge and poor historical understanding of itself? Who should take the responsibility of building the African confidence through beaming the past as a mirror to the future? Africa must tell its story. The blame rest on the shoulders of the older generation and a system that was built to deliberately supplant Africa's original thoughts, beliefs and friendship mechanism appear foolish or non-existent, and make significant population of Africans to be unaware of their heritage and dwelling in the cycle and vision of the African renaissance.

Thomas Sankara I think it was, who says in a paraphrase, 'that a people who do not know their history can be manipulated by anyone'. Let Africans be encouraged to tell their stories, and painstakingly reveal and catalogue historical truth of heroic deed that the black race should celebrate and never forget. Stories of African solidarity, knowledge, leadership and resistance will serve as a fundamental awareness to the history of decolonization of

Africa, and the march towards the African renaissance. It is imperative for every single country in Africa to unveil their historical truth of how the freedom of its people and nations were achieved, especially with the support of other Africans.

Those who experienced the liberation struggle in South Africa may not have passed down the stories and knowledge even orally to their young, and such historical negligence has cost Africa dearly. The inability for South Africans to connect with the real history of the liberation struggle has threatened the gains that could come from the freedom that they have pursue and achieved, but has not materialized into meaningful liberty for the people. No wonder that Lawrence Blum and Victor Seidler (1989), insisted that 'if we have an unreal sense of liberty, our efforts to attain it will be misdirected or, worse, will themselves undermine our aspirations to freedom by generating different and deeper structures of subordination'. It is imperative to find various ways of consolidating the freedom achieved in South Africa by constant recourse to historical truth, in order to conceive a better relationship for a brighter future. That is why more books about friendship, African solidarity and resistance should be written and stories told about how the anti-apartheid movement was won from the perspectives of each single country efforts that contributed in bringing down arguably the most racist administration in Africa's modern history.

PART 2: COLONIALISM BY ANOTHER NAME

Murtala Muhammad making his famous speech against apartheid in 1976

Tebeho Mashinini, the young South African student that led the Soweto uprising

Apartheid in South Africa

I believe in storytelling; stories can change minds, stories can take away dignity and I believe that stories can restore dignity'

Chimamanda Ngozi Adichie

Typical of the stories and account of colonialism in Africa, Europeans have been the major perpetrators of colonization that have influenced a series of events which eventually shaped the political, economic and social landscape of modern South Africa. Apart from the Portuguese and British who have had a historical contact that stimulated the colonial narrative of Southern African countries in general, no other country will influence the milestone of colonialism in South Africa as the Calvinist Dutch of Netherlands and parts of old Germany(W A de Klerk, 1975). The creation of the South African State started with the formation of the Union of South Africa in the year 1910. In the words of Desmond Tutu (1994), 'the Union was formed when two former Afrikaner republics-the South African Republic (the Transvaal) and the Orange Free State, established in the 1850s by descendants of the Dutch, German and French settlers but occupied by the British during the Anglo-Boer war in 1900-joined two British colonies-the Cape Colony and Natal- to create the modern South African state'.

Like other Europeans, exposure to the geographical location called South Africa by the Dutch may have been adventurous or even accidental, but then eventually became commercially profiting, which was the intention of Jan Van Riebeeck, the European character that they claim founded South Africa. The Dutch adventures will follow sequence of deliberate strategies to conquer the original inhabitants that they met in South Africa and capture their factors of production especially their ancestral land, through mostly violent means. It will also follow a deliberate act of self-transformation by the Dutch to forcefully sow themselves in Africa with the hope that they will become a pure breed of white aboriginal in the core of the black race. This implantation of the Dutch in Africa is something that was very distinct and unique to their version and model of colonialism in the continent.

The story was therefore told of some Dutch sailors around the 16th century who were en-route the East Indies and had to stop to refresh along the Cape of Good Hope, an area where the Atlantic meets the Indian Ocean and happen to be the southernmost tip of the African continent before land meets aquatic. These set of Dutch citizens who later preferred to be called Boers (meaning farmers), fell in love with the land that they had dock to replenish so much that they imposed themselves on the native inhabitants, mostly of the Khoi San and Bantu Africans that they met in *Mzansi*. The contact and interactions of the Dutch with the indigenous people kick started a series of events that will alter the development trajectory of both the natives and the European visitors. The natives will experience displacement and will have to suffer centuries of deprivation in a unique amalgam of racially inspired political, economic, and social order of governance orchestrated by the Europeans that will strip the natives of their nationality, dignity, and human rights, and put these local inhabitants at the bottom of the food chain.

The European settlers will over time experience a tremendous development and prosperity from farming, mining and other profitable ventures that will make South Africa a land full of promise. The Boers seem to have come to South Africa on a one-way ticket because their colonial strategy in Africa was such that they expunged the option of going back to their country of origin. There were different versions of why the Dutch came to Africa at that quantifiable time. While some of them were escaping the impact of the Dutch war of independence against Philip II of Spain (W.A de Klerk 1975: pp3-9), another account insisted that they were on a voyage to satisfy their exuberance. Nevertheless, some of these Europeans arrived after stories were told by other sailors who have transverse this nautical route to the East Indies and have beheld the wonder of such beautiful land that will later be called South Africa. The Europeans realized how attractive and blessed the land upon which they trod is. Their desperation to stay, live and build a life for themselves in South Africa made them ruthless in dealing with the natives, and set them on a collision course of belligerence with the British who were part of the colonial history of South Africa. The superior firepower of Britain over these Dutch settlers in what was known as the Anglo-Boer war, gave the Boers the excuse to disperse and move hinterland from the Cape of Good Hope, further disrupting indigenous communities and pillaging the natives along the way.

The movement of the Boers out of Cape Town as a mark of retreat to the British led to the phenomenon called the Voortrekker (the Great Trek), a retreat northward that eventually obligated the Boers to intimidate, subjugate, dehumanize and oppress the indigenous people and communities they find along their path, while reeling under the hype of the Anglo-Boer war. To justify the destruction of the natives and their intention to remain in that area of Africa at all cost, the Boers changed their names to Afrikaner. For the Afrikaner civilization, the stories of the Voortrekker 'was then used to construct an imaginary, divinely-guided Afrikaner community, with a 'Divine' right to dominate, and exert control over local inhabitants (Ebrahim Salie: 2012). The Afrikaans expressed their arrogance and disdain for the cultures, traditions and history of the natives and have done everything in their power to isolate the native cultures through oppressive tendencies, especially for those that have resisted such incursions and narcissism. The strategy of Louis Trichardt 'Great trek' was therefore an annihilation of the history of the indigenous people, a strategy that was somehow adopted many years later at democracy to erase the history and any reference to the contribution and support of other African countries against apartheid.

The Dutch, Boers or Afrikaans depending on how you want to call them were ruthless, they did not bother to convert or Christianized the natives into transforming and becoming like the Dutch, just as was done by the British and or French colonial approach in Africa. The Boers saw themselves as a chosen people saddled with the obligation to breed a pure race of Afrikaners (whatever that means). Thus, the Boers had a short circuit for the resistance put forward by the natives and in response, they just kill, plunder, steal and destroy the spiritual and mundane structure of the natives in order to establish their conquest. The good thing was that the native black majority of the people of Mzansi insisted to firmly keep their identity as deeply African, which in itself was a subtle model of resistance to colonialism.

The initiation of apartheid in South Africa in 1948 by its chief architect Hendrik Verwoerd, ushered in a new form of annexation and a brand of colonialism to the continent of Africa in the middle of the twentieth century. This period coincided with an epoch of global acceptance of human rights, universal freedom and dignity of the human race as the norm of civilized societies and international order. In fact, the same year apartheid regime was instituted was incidentally the same period the United Nations Declaration of Human Rights (UNDHR) was introduced to the world to guide human existence, halt oppression and emphasize the 'fundamental truth that all men are born equal'. Apartheid regime became a contradiction to everything the declaration stood for, and will eventually illustrate apartheid at the insistence of Nigeria, as a crime against humanity and a primitive condition which has no place in modern democracies (Joe Garba, 1996)

Apartheid was a racial configuration and distortion of history and identity of the black majority in South Africa that consequently created a culture of hate, intolerance and under development to a large population of its people. Fortified with a brutal narcissism and resolve never to return to Europe, apartheid crafted by the Boers began a campaign that eliminated the self-worth of the natives in a way that was in contrast to other colonial experience in the continent. This assertion was reinforced by Justin Cartwright in 1977 when he concluded that the Boers and 'the complexities of their motives, the restless nature of their religion, their urge to own land, their familiarity with guns, the commercial aspect of their lives, all these things entail the end of every society they meet'. The Boers became the last active colonial administrators in Africa that did not tie political allegiance to their country of origin, but experimented in undressing and hiding its Caucasian identity deep into the obscure root of Bantu civilization.

The Boers ultimately came to refer themselves as the 'Afrikaneers' and the minority government they instituted were callous regimes orchestrated for uncivilized, undemocratic and roguish administration to pull down anything that stand in their way. They even extended that to the Front-Line States (FLS) who were a collection of majority black African self-governed countries that surrounded South Africa at the time, and went further to plant distrust and enmity among the freedom fighters within Southern Africa. The white minority government in Pretoria denied the native majority their liberty, political and economic rights and even deprived the natives through various policies, from remembering the history of the evil meted on them. It was to this anathema and deliberate but enforced dementia that we shall view the strategy of how a significant history of the liberation struggle got lost to an entire generation inside South Africa after democracy was achieved in 1994. The natives were handed over a society in post- apartheid South Africa that 'comes with the deliberate misrepresentation and erasure of this monumental epoch in the history of black resistance in this country' (David Letsoalo: 2022)

Africa has suffered a history of indignity for centuries at the hands of foreign characters. From slavery to colonialism and everything in-between, it was the redemption and restoration of the value of the black race and everyone on the continent that the concept and content of apartheid became disgusting to the moral, spiritual, physical, emotional and national interest of independent Nigeria. Nigeria fought apartheid with fervent seriousness that was hardly replicated on any continental venture afterwards. It became a moral right of Nigeria to defend and support the liberation struggle by any means necessary to end an arrogant system of institutionalized racism, deprivation and oppression imported into South Africa by foreign elements in their interpretation of expansionism. Quite frankly, it would have been a disgrace if Nigeria just stood by and watch foreigners dehumanize fellow Africans in such a time when it had the moral, political and economic muscles to flex against a system that initiated official racism in Sub Saharan Africa, prohibits the enjoyment of universal freedom and opportunities for the black race.

Apartheid was a child of privilege borne at the twilight of de-colonization in Africa and global political development. The veracity of apartheid that Nigeria could not stand was even made more appalling at a time where universal freedom and international peace was greatly influencing global consensus on democracy, human rights and collective security. Apartheid became a contradiction to egalitarian dogma, an open injury in Africa and while the complacency and hypocrisy of the custodians of democracy in western world could not halt apartheid as was done with the broader notion of slavery, it was to Africans themselves that the responsibility to end apartheid rest.

Nigeria took up such responsibility in cooperation with sister countries, organizations and other 'friends of freedom' across the globe. The execution of such responsibility by Nigeria was so outstanding that it forced a cautious admiration from even the white minority government in Pretoria. Nigerian involvement in the liberation struggle continued to be a thorn in the flesh of the white minority government and had made them uncomfortable throughout the duration that it lasted. The moral commitment manifests itself in Nigeria's persistent support for the oppressed black people in Southern Africa in general and South Africa in particular (Olayiwola Abegunrin; 2009). The contributions of Nigeria to the anti-apartheid movement was acknowledged by some South Africans who admitted the success of such solidarity. A few years back, Major General Daniel Mofokeng, who was Head of SANDF Foreign Relations, said 'the Nigerian government made huge sacrifices for the liberation of South Africa from minority rule (Lebo Keswa: 2015)

Apartheid like other shades of colonialism was supported by the same people, countries and systems that have insisted on equality, liberty and civilized standard of governance. Some of them publicly denounced apartheid but secretly supported it for political, economic, cultural, selfish and racist considerations. Perhaps the apartheid regime in South Africa would have ended sooner than it did, had western countries and governments who frowned at such repressive and discriminatory system of governance honestly and honorably confronted it with the sense of purpose and seriousness that Nigeria exhibited. The apartheid system thrived for so long because nations that should naturally move to overthrow the regime, tolerated it for economic, cultural and strategic gains. This made Africa and in specific term Nigeria, to take upon itself the responsibility to free the black race in the continent of any semblance of white minority oppression of the majority or any form of colonial domination.

Apartheid system was symbolic and planted the diverse multi-racial and ethnic population that had come to be the reality of South

African historical development. The liberation struggle was therefore partly to address the politics of segregation and deprivation where minority are allowed to vote to decide the fate of the majority. This was entrenched without any pretense to the feelings of the African majority, and the Africanist posture of Nigeria's foreign policy could not accept the rationale where about four million whites will determine the fate of fifteen million Africans in South Africa (Emeka Aniagolu:2021). Nigeria saw apartheid as a system that operates under an inconsistent principle that regurgitate an unfair, diabolic and uniquely unacceptable system of colonialism that must be uprooted from the continent.

The component of this level of colonialism in *Mzansi* appealed to the thinking of the white minority regime that without the right to vote by the native majority, it undresses their right to citizenship and monopolized political power in a very unrepresentative way to deprive blacks of their franchise. The motive was stark and the impact of such deprivation did not just supplant the majority right to vote, but also denied them the inalienable right to own land as citizens of a sovereign country. As a matter of fact, the people of Mzansi will continue to see the land question as one of the most fundamental impact of the apartheid system in contemporary times. In any case, this deprivation irritated Nigeria that even the countries who are known propagators of western values and representative democracy like the United States and the United Kingdom will turn a blind eye to the arrogance and hypocrisy of the white minority regime in Pretoria against such international standard of leadership recruitment and livelihood. Nigeria insisted that as far as the liberation struggle persist, equal rights, justice, liberty and inclusive governance must have a universal application in apartheid South Africa.

This became instructive when the growing sentiments of the natives was increasing in the face of alienation by the minority regime in Pretoria. The African majority of South Africa felt like refugees in their own country, alienated from their own land and disadvantaged from accessing the good life, due to the fact that apartheid deprived them of choosing their fate, the freedom to decide the nature of its leadership transformation or the language of instruction and communication in public spaces. The colonial experience in South Africa was multi-dimensional and structural and therefore, exposed the freedom fighters with divergent methods in demanding for true freedom and sense of belonging.

* * *

In retrospect, South Africa or Azania as the freedom fighters or devotees of Robert Sobukwe of the Pan African Congress (PAC) would prefer to call it, emerged from distinct but homogenous nationalities into a country arrangement when the Dutch East India Company set up trading ventures at the tip of the Cape in the busy nautical route through Africa, linking Europe with Asia, at the confluence of the Atlantic and Indian oceans. The nautical relevance of this area soon attracted entrepreneurial ideas which brought a considerable interest in commerce and agriculture activities to meet the need of sailors plying that route on a regular basis. Some among these sailors from the Netherlands opted to stay in the location to build a life for themselves, inspired by the presence of a rich land for agriculture and a climate similar to Europe.

As trade *flourished* in the ever-busy route, some of the Europeans decided to establish farms and ensure food supply to feed crew members as they sail by or dock to refuel. Farming became so lucrative and the lands so pregnant with harvest that it became consequential for more workers in the field to cultivate the land. Caucasians from Europe and workers from the hinterland of Africa and other parts of Asia were brought to work the field and provide for an agricultural boom that will also create the need to expand and acquire more lands in interior spaces. Agriculture was not the only attraction of foreign elements from Europe to pitch tent in South Africa. The discovery of gold, platinum and other precious materials in commercial quantity, expanded the quest for wealth, along with it the desire for power and control.

The European sailors, traders and other field workers brought in as slaves from far away Asia and near, would eventually intermingle and procreate with the Bantu and Khoi-san women who were original inhabitants of the land. This was fostered due to a short supply of women among the field workers as well as the new 'land owners'. Such procreation and integration produced a population of mixed races, whom are a special feature of modern South Africa, but structured in a manner that station the natives at the bottom of the economic tree and disadvantaged in other social indices. Offspring's of Europeans enjoyed privileges of what children of other races could only wish for, and of which intentionally or not, set a precedence of racial hierarchy and segregation that will eventually birth apartheid.

So from around 1652, the colonial adventure or misadventure by Dutch settlers culminated into a sustained regime of conquest and subjugation for centuries that will deliver a firmly established system of apartheid in 1948. Apartheid was a system of separated development where white minority enjoy rights, privileges and development higher than the black majority. It was a unique system of racial supremacy in governance, administration and socio-economic advantage of a few over many. According to Nancy Clark and William Worger (2022), 'by the time apartheid was formally introduced, the core of the system was already laid down by denying Africans in their own ancestral homelands, without the rights to own land, to determine their own government, or even decide where to live or work".

The colonial experience of the people of South Africa followed a deliberate dismantling of everything that gives the natives any advantage or ability for self and collective prosperity, except with a nod from the white minority. The Boers made sure they have legal backing to give legitimacy for their action and coercion. The Group Area Act, Land Amendment Act, the Separate Amenities Act, Bantustan Policy, were all initiated by white minority regimes to consolidate its despicable system of racial discrimination.

Apartheid was a considered system of exploitation perpetuated by a policy of racial hierarchy which gives economic, political, and socio-cultural and community benefit to people based on the color of their skin. The Europeans created this system to exploit opportunities and the growing prospects available in *Mzansi*, at the detriment of the natives. Even before apartheid was officially adopted, the natives were already impoverished as 'only 13% of the land was allocated to majority of blacks, while the white minority were allocated 87% of land' (Emeka Aniagolu: 2021). Land has been the main progenitor that inspired the narrative of colonialism in South Africa.

As the natives became marginalized, deprived, isolated and desolated, the foreigners ate fat from the land, which was literally flowing with milk and honey. Soon enough, the British and Boers inhabitants at this location started creating enclaves over who should control the abundant wealth that South Africa delivers. The Boers now known officially as the Afrikaners had to device so many means to maintain superiority over the natives and have tried in various ways to gain legitimacy of some kind from their new found home and also strained to expunge the impression that they are engaged in colonization in the continent. But it was obvious that apartheid was colonialism by other means.

Such was the story of apartheid in South Africa, a system that became unique in its approach and different from the history of colonial experience of other African countries. The oppressive, discriminatory, tyrannical and evil system that is Apartheid was firmly established the same year people from other climes are basking in the euphoria of new found freedom. It was the same year that the People's Republic of China (PRC) was created out of the ashes of the Cultural Revolution, another liberation struggle that will define the development path of a new China. Ironically, as people of other climes were viewing hope in the horizon that was the same period that the black race in South Africa entered into a renovated colonial experience.

Obtrusively, apartheid removed the flesh of freedom from the native majority and allowed the people to walk in their skeleton so to speak. Apartheid reintroduced a blatant system of dehumanization, oppression, discrimination and deprivation, and the indigenous people who dared to resist the system were crushed in diverse ways using the instruments of state to deny the majority their rights and freedom which the white minority enjoyed without inhibition. Apartheid became a war declared by the minority against the majority, foreign domination against aboriginal culture. It was a limitation forcefully placed on the indigenous people of South Africa by a settler government of white minority that usurped everything that made the native majority humans and empowered. The system of apartheid was as expected resisted by the natives and which came with a lot of casualties.

Apartheid consolidated an institutional racism out of what was the South African Republic, assisted by the presence of the British who had already formed the Union of South Africa. The contention between these two foreigners in 'Mzansi' led to seizure of land from natives that has grossly and disproportionately affected the wealth generation of the people and created feudal system that will come to be a unique shade of colonization in Africa. More so, land was a major factor of production in the country as with the continent at that time, the deprivation of which skewed the natives into the lowest rung of opportunities. As with every unjust system, there was resistance from the natives against the wanton oppression, segregation and discrimination by white minority so much that it bestowed a unique colonial history in South Africa that engulfed the region of Southern Africa.

It is worthy to stress that the system of colonialism in South Africa was different from the experience in other parts of the continent in many logics. Unlike the 'indirect rule' and 'assimilation' systems adopted by the British and French in Africa which ultimately created a center-periphery relationship, to which enabled infrastructure and logistics to move human and material resources out of the continent to develop and benefit their country of origin, the apartheid system in South Africa painstakingly built infrastructure to resettle their kin arriving in droves to Mzansi. Apartheid was also created to maintain hold on political power in perpetuity as a major guarantee for socio-economic dominance of the natives.

Unlike other systems of colonialism, apartheid institutionalized and skewed state capture of political, economic, military, cultural, diplomatic benefits of statecraft on racial ground and consideration. The process of the colonial subjugation of native majority kept changing in definition and refinement since the Great Trek. They initiated this system because they saw how fertile and malaria friendly South Africa is compared to other locations in the continent. It has resources beneath, above and around just like every other place in Africa, but it also has a very clement weather and an escape of tropical diseases that made South Africa worth dying for.

The white visitors refused to leave, and they also won't allow the natives to live in freedom. Unlike the Indirect Rule system or the system of Assimilation used by colonial France and Britain, the case of South Africa was done with no allegiance by the white minority to the country of their origin. The white settlers decided upon contact with South Africa that they are not going to leave, and won't have anything else to do with the Netherland. They even changed their names and identity to cut off any connection with Europe. Apartheid in South Africa became a colonial policy of state capture, which was to dehumanize the host and make them perpetually subservient to the regime.

Again, unlike the Indirect Rule and policy of Assimilation where the colonial perpetrators used the natives of different countries directly or indirectly in the organs and structure of the public sector and governance, apartheid was distinctively exclusionist in policy that used segregation to stop the natives from participating in government. In fact, they were treated like people of no nationality that belong to the lowest rung of everything, not to be seen or heard in the corridors of government or even participate in it, except with permission. It was a system of total discrimination and relegation of the natives to the bottom of the national development hierarchy, and denied of any responsibility to direct their own affairs.

Interestingly, railways and roads were not hurriedly built in South Africa to transport raw materials to the coast for onward sail to Europe, but to serve a growing population of Europeans who have dared to settle and build a life in a fascinating part of Sub-Saharan Africa endowed with possibilities. The apartheid system was a settler administration with no intention of leaving Africa back to their original abode. As the political, social and economic dynamics in South Africa have revealed, the structure put on ground during apartheid was to permanently perpetuate white minority government in the country, but shade it with colors that may not be too obvious as a colonial administration.

South Africa, a Nation in Distress

The unique location and the wealth underneath, on land and above South Africa has everything to do with why white minority Europeans controlled the governments and coveted the land to themselves against the odds. South Africa was where other white minority regimes in Southern Africa be it Northern or Southern Rhodesia, ran to cluster during decolonization campaign in the region, when indigenous governments and black majority took over power. South Africa during this period of the liberation struggle became the only enclave where the white minorities from every other place came to gather, or they had nowhere else to go, except to leave the continent-which was not an option for some of them, especially the Afrikaneers.

Also, unlike its northern neighbors Zimbabwe, South Africa is not a tropical space and enjoys a fascinating weather condition that Europeans find appealing to their lifestyle, agronomy and health. Many came to love South Africa due to its weather and unique pastures which feels like the one in Europe and supports more 'exotic' food, lifestyle and plants like no other in the continent. No Caucasian who came to South Africa before the liberation struggle or after would want to leave or does not have fond memories of its great attributes. The love for this unique space in Africa as earlier stated was worth dying for by the Afrikaneers and eventually, they subdued native inhabitants to retain advantage over the resources that the land rears. However, there is no way that you can suppress and marginalize a people for so long and don't expect a revolt.

During the apartheid regime which lasted more than five decades, so much atrocities and pillage were done against the original communities and inhabitants. In order to retain the system that only benefit white minority governments and its European relatives against an impoverished majority of black Africans, the white minority regimes were brutal to black resistance. The apartheid government did everything within its capacity to shut out South Africa from the rest of the world, even closing South Africa to other African countries who eventually got independence and were demanding an end to the racially political, economic and cultural repression of which apartheid epitomize in the continent. The way other African governments and people went about fighting apartheid was done both on individual and collective terms. But the majority people of South Africa did not get the privilege of knowing so much about these efforts by other Africans, because the white minority government in Pretoria isolated them from their African kin.

It was not surprising to see several resistances against apartheid from the African majority who could not continue to live in servitude on their ancestral land. Whether it was from King Shaka, King Moshoeshoe or others who came later, the people of Mzansi have been known to seek freedom in their ancestral land and this was done by fighting against foreign invasion. Those of the freedom fighters who took over the fight for freedom from the monarchies against the invasion of their country like John Dube and Isaka Seme among others, became more strategic and organized as they would later convene a meeting to establish the South Africa Native National Congress, which later became the ANC. The ANC became the vehicle for the redemption and freedom of the oppressed people of Mzansi.

Inspired by the anti-colonialist before them, and convinced by the natural principle that all men (and women) desire freedom in all circumstance, Africans like Seme, Dube, Lithuli, OR Tambo, Walter Sisulu, Mandela, Desmond Tutu, etc. thought differently from the warrior posture of Monarchs of the past. These conscious personalities started what was to be known as the non-violent resistance to colonial authority and the brutal system of apartheid. They adopted strategies along peaceful means of ending the oppressive and discriminatory system. But like every struggle with changing perspective and interest, the liberation struggle could no longer remain peaceful without the threat or use of the instruments of violence, following historical accounts.

The youth wing of the ANC and more specifically the Umkhonto we Sizwe (MK) was created for such a reason as to pick up arms against apartheid where necessary. The inspiration was drawn from other liberation movement in history which has to be won through armed struggles, coercion and militancy, not by just civil disobedience. Even before the youth wing started applying any option of violence, the apartheid regime and their collaborators have designated the ANC, PAC and other freedom fighters as terrorist organizations. Such nomenclature was resisted vehemently by Nigeria which seized every opportunity to publicly denounce such label on the freedom fighters. Such denouncement by Nigeria and other such effrontery helped to win understanding and sympathies from the international community, even among western alliance who initially thought that the fight for freedom by the oppressed people of South Africa was instigated by a communist country or agenda. Freedom was and has always been a human need and a tool for living a fulfilled life.

The search for freedom and African resistance against apartheid came to be collectively described as the anti-apartheid movement and was expressed in the liberation struggle. The liberation struggle was fought on two main fronts. There were those who fought apartheid from within South Africa itself, whose resistance were brazen and perpetually in opposition with the white minority government in deed and words inside the sovereignty of the South African state. The second front of the resistance was fought by those in exile. The exiled who fought from outside the territory of South Africa will come to play one of the most significant role in the liberation struggle. It was to these group of people that the mobilization of support and resources, succor and grit could get to the liberation fighters within South Africa. The exiled especially are the custodians of knowledge of the chaos going on within and the window by which support from outside were organized and disbursed.

Just like many liberation struggles, the struggle to attain liberty by the oppressed was resisted by the oppressor, in this case the white minority governments in Pretoria and others who profit from such domination. The apartheid regime came down hard on voices calling for equality, justice, self-determination and freedom. The white minority governments gagged the people from screaming out loud against the evil of apartheid and have many people mysteriously disappeared or killed. They also closed South Africa from external interference, scrutiny or support that could come from other countries in solidarity with the liberation struggle. Shutting South Africa to the world produced two results that favored the apartheid regime. It enabled apartheid to flourish for decades without external interference and eliminated any chance of the native majority getting their stories out there and getting help. For the period apartheid lasted, it also produced in perpetuity an oblivious people who do not know what others were doing outside their borders in their favor.

Many who resisted the discriminatory system of apartheid within South Africa like Mr. Bantu Steve Biko and Solomon Mahlangu and many like them, died for the struggle, some jailed and a great number flee to other countries to seek asylum. The oppressive reality of apartheid would insist on some of its prominent freedom fighters like OR Tambo, Nelson Mandela, Thabo Mbeki, Miriam Makeba, and many others to proceed on self-exile in self-preservation and effective engagement. Being on exile accorded some of them a strategic responsibility to chart a direction for the eventual defeat of apartheid. Some of these category of asylum seekers will come to play a profound role in the liberation struggle and open a vista to the nature, approach and assistance that the liberation struggle would enjoy from far and near.

Note earlier that the strategies used to fight apartheid was two edged. From within South Africa, the freedom fighters sustained a concerted revolt, civil disobedience and labor strikes by workers and ordinary citizens which undermined revenues and stability that the white settler government required to fund and facilitate the minority regime. On the other side, there were also pressures mounted by native South Africans on exile as well as countries like Nigeria and the 'friends of freedom' to isolate Pretoria from the comity of nations as their conduct contradicts the tenets of internationally acceptable democratic principles. The leadership structure to fight apartheid was divided into two, those who planned and executed the fight from inside South Africa, and those who planned and executed it from exile. Nigeria made sure that these two approaches aligned. Nigeria sponsored many South Africans on exile to acquire education and create awareness and any other means to ensure that the liberation struggle does not wax cold. Nigeria sponsored international pressure to be brought down heavily on Pretoria through economic isolation and sanctions, blockade to access loans from international finance institutions (IFI), labor strikes and demonstrations against apartheid became sporadic and persistent across the world.

The "exiled" played a prominent role in interfacing with the 'friends of freedom' across the globe and such engagement had a profound impact on ending apartheid. The erroneous impression that some of the 'exiled' were cowardly or a sell-out who ran out of Mzansi when the going was rough and tough, was deciphered in bad faith. Some of the most illustrious freedom fighters during the liberation struggle had to leave to raise capital and the needed awareness of the distressing human conditions that the natives were faced with, without which many people would have been unaware. Even the remarkable influencers of the liberation struggle and stalwarts of ANC like Oliver Tambo, Thabo Mbeki, and others like Miriam Makeba and Tebeho Mashinini had to flee in order to stay alive and escape the credible threat to their lives within South Africa, or to become more effective in seeking support from diaspora in ending the brutal and oppressive regime that was brought to bear in *Mzansi*.

In fact, it was to these group of people that credit of knowing the evil that was going on within South Africa will be understood. These group of exiled South Africans will tell the stories and eventually mobilize support for the liberation struggle and influence the outcome of the struggle as much as those who fought from within the country. The exiled kept the flame of the liberation struggle burning as this was necessary to those fighting from within to gain momentum, even to those either incarcerated in prisons for life or incapacitated by the oppressive regime. The apartheid government hunted down its critics even outside its sovereignty. South Africa during such period became too hot for meaningful engagement, and too dangerous for any effective and sensible dialogue with the racist regime.

One of the countries within Africa that stood by the oppressed people of South Africa during the liberation struggle and feature prominently by engaging with the freedom fighters both within and the 'exiled' was Nigeria. The contribution of Nigeria will eventually sustain and encourage the liberation struggle towards a logical end. It is therefore unfortunate that such collaboration could not even be mentioned in citadels of learning and knowledge hubs. The absenteeism of historical facts by which many Africans know themselves is causing unnecessary friction in the continent. A lot of people within South Africa do not know much about the liberation struggle and this has openly or covertly created some contradictions in intra African relations. According to Attahiru Jega (2010), 'the contradictions, constraints, and inherent weaknesses are glaringly manifest; hence the urgent need to strengthen and re-evaluate policy in line with the requirements of a fast changing and rapidly globalizing world'. One of the requirement will be to include African history in building a knowledge base that will support African political, social, economic, spiritual and philosophical atmosphere for sustainable development. Knowledge should drive progress and without a deliberate step to uphold such knowledge, a country or region could take on a random character that is not supported by its unique ancient wisdom.

Narrating the Afrocentric version of the liberation struggle is vital to create a paradigm shift and decolonize education in Africa. South Africa after apartheid is expected to build and sustain a rich history of Africanism. Keeping a rich document of African history to native South Africans is necessary because making people forget their history was a deliberate endeavor by the white minority government in Pretoria to keep the people of Mzansi in perpetual state of ignorance, inequality and inertia, while they build the livelihood of white privileges and remaking their own history in apartheid and post-apartheid South Africa.

Africa; Call to Action

A novel reason for the growing discontent over the racist regime in South Africa was the advent of political independence that swept across Africa. When many countries emerged out of the ashes of colonialism to political freedom, so was the number of voices calling for the end of apartheid, especially that the consortium of white ruled governments in Southern Africa started reducing with the independence and political freedom of Mozambique, Zimbabwe, Angola and later Namibia. It was on this ground that when countries in Africa gained independence from colonial rule and had established the direction of its destiny, that there was a moral imperative by many of them to step into the embarrassing situation apartheid had imposed on Africans in South Africa, where the Africans are oppressed, subjugated and made to work akin to slaves, in order to build a paradise for the white minority Europeans. While the resources and energies of the natives are exploited to provide enormous comfort for the white, the native majority were forced to live in paucity and inhumane conditions.

Nigeria was by intent and purpose one of the prominent countries in Africa that made a monumental inscription to the liberation struggle by the mandate of its foreign policy. Nigeria's overall policy towards South Africa was derived strictly from its firm and total commitment to achieve accelerated decolonization and to uphold the dignity of the black race (Olayiwola Abegunrin: 2009). It was on this ground that Nigeria 'made the most prodigious and robust contribution to the anti-apartheid movement compared to any other African country, besides the Southern African countries directly involved in the white settler phenomena on the African continent' (Emeka Aniagolu:2021). The Africanist posture of Nigeria foreign policy thrust gave successive governments in Nigeria the impetus to place Africa and the countries within the region at the center-piece of its engagement with any foreign element. Whether it serves Nigeria's immediate national interest or not, Nigeria have been known to mobilize against any interest that stands contrary to the hopes and aspirations of African countries individually or collectively. For about three decades up to 1994 when majority rule and democracy replaced apartheid in South Africa, Nigeria played a pivotal role in setting agendas, ideals, actions and deliberation that would have otherwise been difficult to make by other African countries over the South African question. There were hardly any open or clandestine overtures by the friends of freedom in Africa that didn't admit the strategic importance of the support given by the people and government of Nigeria.

It was with the South African question that for the first time and perhaps the last in recent memory, that the aspirations of all Nigerian citizens aligned with the position of their government regarding the annihilation of the white minority government and system of apartheid in Mzansi. This support by Nigerians to its government towards the oppressed people of South Africa was neck deep and came from a place of love and sense of African comradeship. Such massive support to get involved in the liberation movement was an impetus that the Nigerian government needed, and the legitimacy required to sound the buzzer for Nigeria and rest of Africa to stand up to its responsibility of confronting the oppressive and racist system of apartheid in the motherland. The call to rise against apartheid became louder in Nigeria by the 1970s and was answered by many African countries to the dismay of the white minority government in Pretoria.

Although apartheid thrived for decades before the period covered in this book, some recourse to years back shows that Nigeria have been involved in the liberation struggle as soon as Nigeria got her independence. A good example of the role Nigeria played during the liberation struggle was to shield Nelson Mandela from arrest and offer him sanctuary when there was an international manhunt for Mr. Mandela by the South African security and intelligence services.

Mr. Nelson Mandela was offered refuge by the Nigerian government and he stayed for six months in No 5, Okotie Eboh Street, Ikoyi, Lagos state. He was accommodated for that duration by Chief Madubike Ameachi in his official residence in 1963. As Chief Ameachi recalled, 'Mandela came to stay with me on the request of Dr. Nnamdi Azikiwe, the then Governor General of Nigeria'. Nigeria knew that the British and South African intelligence officers were looking to arrest Mandela and other ANC leaders and they brought Mandela to Nigeria so he could keep a low profile before the warrant on him could wane.

However, Mandela in his unfolding leadership qualities at that time, decided to return back to South Africa because according to him, 'he could not in good conscience, continue to hide from the oppressors when thousands of his people are going through the evil of apartheid inside South Africa'. Mandela put the demands of his people before his safety and thought that his people needed him now more than ever and he returned to South Africa and was later arrested and tried through a kangaroo court and sentenced to life imprisonment.

There were several group and organizations that sprang up in Nigeria all in the bid to show Nigerian solidarity to native South Africans during apartheid and to actualize the decolonization of South Africa. Millions of young Nigerians demonstrated in tertiary institutions, while public servants openly supported the course in various ways. Thousands of school children and young adults in Nigeria were obsessively involved in the call and response to the liberation struggle in forming clubs and association to constantly put the anti-apartheid movement in the front pages of daily-news at various schools and universities. Young Nigerians established the Youth Solidarity for Southern Africa (YUSSA) as a direct response to put pressure and lobby opinion leaders and government officials in Nigeria to make it a policy that liberation struggle must be at the priority list of Nigerian government and national interest. Such efforts generated a lot of interest to end apartheid.

The Nigerian Labour Congress (NLC) was also deeply and strategically involved in supporting the liberation struggle during the Murtala/Obasanjo regimes, by providing training and cooperating with the members of the Congress of South African Trade Unions (COSATU). The NLC and other Trade Unions in Nigeria supported the liberation struggle in different forms. The NLC worked closely with Mark Tshope, who was the COSATU representative in Nigeria around the period of 1978, to support and increase the morale of civil society union in South Africa to fight the discriminatory incarnations of apartheid towards black South African workers, boldly supported by the Nigerian National Action

Committee against Apartheid (NACAP). The NACAP was established to coordinate Nigeria's response to apartheid and channel the support of the people of Nigeria to native South Africans both inside and outside Mzansi.

One of the most remarkable reactions of the NLC and Trade Union Congress of Nigeria in support of the liberation struggle was in the visit of former British Prime Minister, Margret Thatcher to Nigeria in 1987. Before her visit to Nigeria, Margret Thatcher was in South Africa, and flew from there to Nigeria on an African tour of the first female Prime Minister of the United Kingdom. The NLC organized a demonstration to protest the lackluster position or maybe even tacit support by the British government to apartheid South Africa. The demonstration started in Lagos and was supported by the National Association of Nigerian Students (NANS) and the people of Nigeria, and was led by the NLC and participated by individuals like SG Ikoku, who was the Chairman of NACAP. The protest in Lagos was obsessively manic, the motorcade of Margret Thatcher was pelted and people burnt the Union Jack flag while the British Prime Minister stared in disbelief of the potent anger her visit to Nigeria ignited.

If she thought the demonstration that greeted her and the chaos it generated was over in Lagos, she was surprised at what she found in the ancient city of Kano when she visited as well. Salisu Nuhu Mohammed was the former acting general secretary of the NLC at the time, and he organized the demonstration in Kano against the visit of the British Prime Minister to the city, and Kano never witnessed a demonstration of its kind after that. The Kano demonstration in solidarity with the people of South Africa was so militant that it almost overwhelmed the security arrangement to ensure the safety of the British Prime Minister. Margret Thatcher was shocked to her bone marrow at the solidarity protest against apartheid that erupted and she was visibly shaken. The impact was so strong that after she returned to London, the decision to release Mandela became her priority.

The demonstrations in Lagos and Kano were not accidental. Nigeria's foreign policy direction would provide the impetus for sustaining the excitement of political independence across Africa and build a consciousness that helped the liberation struggle in the 1970s, 1980s and 1990s. Along with independence also came the enormous responsibilities of taking care of the collective destiny of the people and charting a path of development that will make the independent African countries responsible players in global affairs. The political leadership of Nigeria ensured that the country adopts an Africanization posture in relation to South Africa and any dealings and pronouncement of Nigeria in regional bodies like the Organization of African Unity (OAU), which transformed into the African Union (AU). Nigeria put itself into the diplomatic circle of the AU and UN with panache and pulled the weight of several African countries on its shoulders.

The near obsessive dedication by the Nigerian state and its people to eliminate apartheid from the continent will later reveal in the number of times that Nigeria led the United Nations Special Committee against Apartheid (UNSCA), an intervention of the UN created at the behest of Nigeria in order to address the evil of apartheid in South Africa, a responsibility of which Nigeria held with fixated attention. Such responsibility required Nigeria to reach out and work with governments and people of shared moral standing against apartheid, and even rebuff friends and allies who showed sympathy to the evil regime of oppression and exploitation that apartheid symbolized.

Ending apartheid was a responsibility that Nigeria successfully executed against all odds. For the Nigerian leadership and its people, "we consider it to be our duty, thrust on us by history and by our subscription to the universally accepted principles of justice and fair play, to keep up and extend the campaign against the racist regime in Pretoria until the apartheid structure on which it rest collapse" (Ibrahim Babangida 1991:252). The Nigerian people and government were in united in purpose and the call to dismantle apartheid in South Africa.

The Africa centered foreign policy focus that energized Nigeria foreign policy actually manifested and got expression from the liberation struggle. The big brother role Nigeria played to end apartheid or any form of foreign political domination in Africa are evident in Southern Africa. There could be different argument to this, but the role Nigeria played in the liberation struggle had generated substantial debates on whether there was any consideration for Nigeria national interest in the enormous contributions it made to the struggle. In fact, after almost three decades of democracy in South Africa to which Nigeria helped to install, deliberations on whether Nigeria was ever in the picture of the liberation struggle have become a recurring decimal in contemporary discourse on Nigeria- South Africa relations.

It was no secret that for the sake of liberating the people of South Africa from the clutches of white minority rule, Nigeria had no choice but to either be in confrontation with erstwhile friends or allies, lost substantial financial benefits for supporting the anti-apartheid movement, or had to bear the responsibilities of the liberation struggle above any other in Africa. Nigeria rolled up its sleeve and got to work in a very conscious and deliberate fashion to eradicate apartheid by any means available. That few documentary evidences are available in South Africa to tell versions of Nigeria contributions to the liberation struggles does not change the fact that Nigeria was a major positive stimulus on how apartheid was toppled in South Africa.

The dedication to the liberation struggle made Nigeria the longest charge d' affairs country to serve as the Chair of the UN Special Committee against Apartheid, a responsibility it executed with admirable professionalism and purpose. In 1982 while still the Chair of the Special Committee, the UN declared an international year of mobilization for sanctions against apartheid South Africa. Through the call for collective action, Nigeria and other members of the UN have recognized the threat to international peace and security which apartheid regime represents, and the destabilizing role it created in Southern Africa and within the FLS.

During the liberation struggle and the decades under focus in this book, Africa experienced a profound group consciousness that transcended many of the faultiness that the continent currently deals with. It was a journey of Africa's ignition into the devoutness of black distinctiveness of what Africa stands for, and how it intends to contribute to human progress. It was the period of Pan-Africanism at its potent stage. The manifestation of such potency was to prove that Africans can unite in words and action to resist what is inimical to its over-all interest.

This call to action was imminently a tool to test the sincerity of countries on international morality and support for a fair and just world. Nigeria through the UN as a global emerging authority persuaded other countries to enlist for sanction on South Africa. A result that came out of this mobilization was increased awareness throughout the world to speak and call for global cooperation to end injustice and restore the dignity of indigenous people. It led to altering public opinion on action to isolation for the apartheid regime. The mobilization campaign was a success as it produced sustained pressure and awareness of the inhuman treatment of natives that even the Netherlands, the country of origin on which the 'Mothership' that sailed to South Africa in the sixteen century and culminated into apartheid had to cut ties with their kindred in South Africa.

Significant among countries who played direct and strategic roles along with Nigeria within the continent are the FLS. These countries are mostly those whom also gained independence and are located in Southern Africa region, most of them sharing boundaries with South Africa. The FLS also enjoyed enormous support from Nigeria during their fight to gain political freedom for their own people as well. Nigeria and some FLS had already familiar relations that will assist in the acceleration to bring down apartheid in South Africa. Other friends of freedom who supported the liberation struggle with a vehement determination outside of Africa were some countries of the global south like India, Brazil, and China. There was huge support that also came from the Nordic countries, especially Sweden. Pressure groups and other influential bodies sprang up from even within countries whose governments were not disposed to ending apartheid, but of which some of its citizens developed their own moral judgment to the South African question, a huge thanks to Nigeria's determined awareness campaigns.

The collaboration between Nigeria and the FLS was very influential to the liberation struggle on a regional scale and even internationally, that it helped in bringing political freedom and majority government to Angola and Namibia. The contribution of Nigeria was so profound that even though not geographically located in Southern Africa, Nigeria was considered a FLS. While Pretoria was exploiting its economic dominance in Southern Africa to control and dictate outcomes of the policies of decolonization coming from the FLS, Nigeria was bidden to flex its economic muscles to assist the FLS stay focus within its resources to ending apartheid, as well as balance the power dynamics of South Africa and the FLS.

It should still be in our memories that the successive white minority governments in South Africa made life very difficult for the governments of the FLS. Waging wars of destabilization and economic sabotage was a strategy Pretoria used to keep the FLS in a choke-hold, especially in Botswana, Mozambique, Namibia and a large extent Angola, while exploiting the resources of these countries to maintain its influence in the region. Nigeria became the only African country in the period that could credibly counter such power that the White minority government had on the region, especially as it concerns socio-economic dynamics of the liberation struggle. In fact, part of the success Nigeria could outline of its contribution during the liberation struggle was the political and economic influence it was able to wield in drawing international solidarity to make apartheid too expensive a system for Pretoria to sustain, and also serve as a balancing power for the FLS.

The confrontation with South Africa and other western powers for the sake of the liberation struggle had even threatened to undermine the economic advantage of Nigeria, but Nigeria's involvement in the fight for freedom of this particular class of Africans was a task that must be done. For Nigeria, the liberation struggle was a political measure that came with a severe geo-strategic, economic, social and security implications to its internal polity. Nigeria had to confront capitalism and its agents, a system that it was adhering and benefiting from since independence in both domestic and international frontage, but the necessity of ridding South Africa of white minority government became superseding and brought it on a collision course with hitherto allies and friends, just for the sake of majority South Africans and indeed international peace.

These facts could be contested by any who may have some reservations on the historical accounts herein. But no matter how varied opinions on this may be, there is no contest that Nigeria's role in the liberation struggle in South Africa in particular, and Southern Africa in general, had one of the most remarkable influences in ending the settler regime in that region. The success in ending apartheid was a result of cooperation and determination by the South African freedom fighters themselves, and the people and government of Nigeria to see equal rights and justice prevail inside South Africa. The implementation of such noble quest in the liberation struggle may have generated disagreement or antagonism from the very people who should be the beneficiaries of its success, however. It was this assertion that generated several theories on the intrigue and politics that shrouded the liberation struggle between actors like the African National Congress (ANC), Pan African Congress (PAC) and other factions involved in the fight for freedom.

It will be grossly invaluable however, to erase the significant contributions made by Nigeria, and many other African countries to see the end of apartheid in the continent.

Nevertheless, Nigeria became aware that ridding South Africa of apartheid and its evil exploitation is a task that must be achieved by any means necessary. This was even the consensus at the regional level, when the former OAU declared support for the liberation struggle. It was a call to duty for every independent African country to support in their own and practical ways to end the colonialism in the continent. Nigeria regarded apartheid as a crime against humanity. Nigeria treated this notion with utmost seriousness. The proximity of these FLS to South Africa became necessary as a buffer and an area of coordination for the liberation struggle. Nigeria made sure that the FLS do not relent in their responsibility, and cultivated a robust support system with them to ensure that the objective of the liberation struggle was achieved without limitation to material, financial and moral burden to the FLS. The cooperation between Nigeria and the FLS presented a common front and unity of purpose that showed that Africa had woken up to the call of its ancestors to be each other's support system. It was a united effort of African resistance against colonization.

*   *   *

Nigeria never wasted any opportunity to expose the evil of apartheid on global, regional, or local platforms. The Festival of Black Arts and Culture hosted in 1977 also known as FESTAC '77 held in Lagos was a platform that Nigeria exploited to rally African artist and cultural ambassadors against apartheid. It promoted a strong level of awareness and a sense of solidarity among Africans and the world at large, and beam even brighter the searchlight against marginalization and oppression. Those who didn't know or even cared about the injustice and human indignity of native South Africans, became aware by the call to actions of prominent musicians, artist and what will today be termed social media influencers. Nigeria identified the impact of arts and music to social transformation.

Nigerian musical artists in particular wrote hit songs promoting solidarity with the African majority in South Africa, some of these songs were in collaborations with South African artists themselves. Miriam Makeba was given unfettered access into Nigeria and she was supported in every conceivable way to campaign against apartheid using music, and call for the abolition of the oppressive system, while also calling for global support for the freedom fighters within South Africa. One of the most prolific takeout of the FESTAC 77, thanks to the platform in creating awareness through the arts against apartheid, was the power and opportunity that music holds in social justice and positive change.

As Chair of the UNSCA however, Nigeria made sure that they countered the narrative brewing in the western hemisphere that native South Africans were incapable of ruling themselves and were terrorist that must be restrained. This narrative greatly impacted on the positive response and responsibility that some western nations could have given to the apartheid imbroglio in South Africa. Somewhere in the charade, the US and UK made the liberation struggle looked like an ideological East versus West issue, that the liberation movement was a communist agenda. They misinformed their citizens to think that the liberation struggle was nothing short of misguided people used by the Soviet Union to wrestle power from a capitalist-oriented government in Pretoria, of which America is one of its biggest trading partners.

Nigeria knew that they had a huge task in public awareness of changing the propaganda and misinformation already in circulation in the western hemisphere. A good job they did by collaborating with black movement organizations in the US to paint the true picture of the injustice and dehumanization going on in South Africa against not only the natives, but other minority nationalities that have come to call that great country their home. Many conferences and seminars were organized and papers delivered, speeches made and better understanding of the issues was achieved. Majority of these conferences were solely organized by Nigeria. Nigerian diplomats and representatives spoke eloquently to audiences in France, Britain and the United States which included parliamentarians, politicians, students and pressure groups among many.

One of the biggest successes of Nigeria as a country and as Chair of the Special Committee was the launch of a massive international awareness campaign in countries like France, the UK, US, the Nordic states and Arab countries. Such awareness brought light to the true nature of the apartheid policies on native majority of South Africans and the threat apartheid pose to humanity and international peace and security. A great deal of people eventually came to see apartheid as nothing to do with the cold war, but lust for power and inherent quest of man to dominate another by brute force and reckless adventurism. That was the reason why many countries came to support the works of the UN Special Committee which Nigeria made possible even when the US, the UK and France refused to join the UN Special Committee to make sure that the UN described apartheid for what it is; evil.

The 1970s, 1980s and 1990s are by far Nigeria most active period of the liberation struggle as noted earlier. This is not to dismiss its contribution to the liberation movement in the prior decade. After the civil war and other political and economic challenges it faced in the 1960s, Nigeria bounced back to join the decolonization movement sweeping across Africa with keen interest on the liberation struggle and with a renewed vigor, strategy and tenacity. The resolve to end apartheid became Nigeria's only national interest for so long that when majority rule was finally achieved and democracy enthroned in South Africa, Nigeria had a hard time readjusting and realigning its Africanist foreign policy with her national interest in post-apartheid South Africa.

PART 3: NIGERIA AND THE POWER OF DIPLOMACY

Commonwealth Eminent Persons Group with Olusegun Obasanjo and Chief Emeka Anyaoku, discussing the release of Mandela and ending apartheid

Joe Garba, Former Nigerian Permanent Representative and Chairman of the United Nations Special Committee against Apartheid

Africa Has Come of Age

'We must learn to live the African way. It's the only way to live in freedom and with dignity'.

Thomas Sankara

Before the wave of independence swept across Africa in the 1960s, the continent had already been blessed with enormous human and natural resources that gives the promise of a brighter future. Africans were already firmly established in philosophy, prolific in administration and classical realism, resolute in leadership and the direction that the continent should take to become a great expanse. Nigeria as a country could boast of intellectuals and founding fathers like Nnamdi Azikiwe, Tafawa Balewa, Obafemi Awolowo, Herbert Macaulay, Ahmadu Bello, Funmilayo Ransome-Kuti, Anthony Enahoro, etc. There were also contributions of military leaders in Nigeria like General Yakubu Gowon, General Murtala Mohammed, General Olusegun Obasanjo and Major General Joseph Garba among other names, to which stories of the liberation struggle in Nigeria won't be complete. Even the civil society, labor unions and the academia made giant contributions to developing and sustaining the momentum that gave Nigeria a unique position in the history of the liberation struggle in South Africa. Coupled with the capacity and sheer brilliance of anti-colonial personalities from other sister countries like Kwame Nkrumah of Ghana, Julius Nyerere of Tanzania, Amical Cabral of Guinea Bissau, Kenneth Kaunda of Zambia, Ahmed Sekou Toure of Guinea, Bantu Steve Biko, Robert

Sobukwe, Thabo Mbeki of South Africa, Samora Machel of Mozambique, Seretse Khama of Botswana, the list just goes on. These set of foundational leadership that Africa had, were also transferred to reformers much younger but more resolute in their determination to see Africa stand on its feet.

The creation of the Organization of Africa Unity (OAU) which later became African Union (AU) was a testament to a prolific genius of African leadership that were all part of the journey of minds and energies towards an independent and purposeful tour into collective greatness as a continent. Nigeria at every level even after its civil war that started in 1967 and ended in 1970, kept a keen eye on the progress and trials of sister countries. The leadership direction Nigeria gave to Africa was felt within and outside its borders, right through continental spaces. During one of such periods in 1976, African leaders converged in Addis Ababa to proffer ways and means to challenges confronting the continent and in particular the issue of colonialism and independence of African countries still under the yoke of white minority administrations. That year became a watershed moment for Nigeria again to take up its leadership role in fighting the evil of apartheid. The famous speech delivered by General Murtala Muhammed at an extraordinary summit of the OAU on 11th January 1976, impressed all those present and echoed across the globe, as well as reclaimed back the confidence of African leaders to a common objective.

The speech reiterated that Africa will not stand by and watch foreigners decide how Africans run themselves. This was assumed to be in response to letters sent to African leaders by the then US President Gerald Ford who insisted and warned African leaders to toe the line of caution by not interfering or supporting the anti-apartheid movement and liberation struggle which according to the US president, 'this struggle is being planned and executed by terrorist cum communist organizations'. General Murtala Muhammed could not hide his disagreement to such assertion by the US President which he expressed at the extraordinary session of the OAU on that faithful day. The speech contradicted the US President's position about the liberation struggle with no apology, and also indicated how serious the Nigerian Head of Government and by extension, African leaders are poised to protect the people of Southern Africa who are living under colonial subjugation and apartheid.

Nigeria insisted that the time has come when Africans should make it clear to the international community that Africa can decide and think for itself, "that we know our own interest and how to protect those interest; that we are capable of resolving African problems without presumptuous lessons in ideological dangers which, more often than not, have no relevance for us, nor for problems at hand". General Murtala Muhammed went further to insist that 'Africa should no longer take orders from any country, however powerful, as nobody should tell us who should be our friends'.

This speech by the Nigerian leader which left no one in doubt that Nigeria has locked horns with the US over apartheid South Africa, became global newsflash. It was rumored that the hardline support by Nigeria to the liberation struggle in 1976 and the doggedness of the Nigeria government at that time to confront any country that supports the oppression of native South Africans got General Murtala Muhammed killed. Barely four weeks after making that inspiring and thought-provoking speech in Addis Ababa and matching those words with action by refusing the aircraft carrying American Secretary of State Henry Kissinger to land in Nigeria, General Murtala Muhammed was 'taken out' as a result. The support Nigeria provided to the liberation struggle was uncompromising and yet successful as it led eventually to freedom and independence in Angola and Namibia, and reignited the vigor in motion for self-determination to end apartheid completely in South Africa.

So much attention was brought to light over the South African question in Murtala Muhammed speech that after the meeting in Addis Ababa, the speech shifted attention of the world to Nigeria and the leadership it has once again assumed in Africa. Murtala Muhammed resolutely declared that Africa has come of age to decide for itself how to shape its future and superintend over its affairs. He went further to show how serious the government and people of Nigeria was, when he constituted one of the brightest and target-oriented team of Nigerians in both the military and diplomatic services, to make sure that apartheid see the fiercest opposition to its existence on the continent. Nigeria made personal sacrifices in its resolve to end apartheid by providing necessary human resources and finances which became one of the watershed moments in the liberation struggle.

Most instructive was the significance of the decisive and purpose driven leadership provided by Murtala and later by the Obasanjo government that left even the hardened pessimist of the quality of African leadership during such period to admit that Africa has truly come of age and could handle its affairs. Back then, the Nigerian leaders governed impressively and with resolve. One of such resolve shocked the international community. Who would have thought that the government of Nigeria for the sake of the liberation struggle, and to prove Nigeria's disparity with the US over American position on the South African question, will refuse to allow the aircraft of the charismatic US Secretary of state Henry Kissinger to land in Lagos? The refusal to give the green light for landing the plane of the famous American diplomat astonished the international community, and the more incredulous was that this stern decision by Nigeria was done in protest on behalf of the oppressed people of South Africa.

Nigeria's resolve to end apartheid relentlessly was emphasized and witnessed in planned and sometimes sporadic navigation, all in the bid to show firm commitment to the liberation struggle. For instance, the nationalization of multi-national corporations belonging to key super powers in the world, the sanctions and boycott of major global events initiated by Nigeria against South Africa, and the loudest voice in the room against apartheid on many international gathering, made Nigeria an unmistakable leader of the anti-apartheid movement in not only Africa, but globally . The audacity shown by the Nigerian leadership against apartheid and every perceived supporter of the white minority regime in Pretoria left no individual, group and country in doubt that Nigeria is completely serious to match word with action over apartheid. That gesture sent shockwaves across the international community. Even the Soviet Union was perplexed to a jaw dropping amazement at the audacity and will of Nigeria's government to fight against all those who supported apartheid.

It was therefore a never seen before act of defiance to have occurred in the diplomatic circle as a Nigeria Head of State, General Murtala

Muhammed stood up to the US by denying to see an already descending plane into Nigerian airspace of the highly respected Secretary of State Henry Kissinger, on the grounds of the moral support America still provide at the time, to apartheid South Africa. No African country in that epoch could have dared to do that. It was a huge embarrassment to America to the bewilderment of many observers of international relations and politics. That episode was one of the most historic gestures of support Nigeria gave to the liberation struggle. It was believed that General Murtala Muhammed short stay as the military Head of Government of Nigeria was over his position in the anti-apartheid movement. He paid with his life for the audacity in leadership he displayed for the liberation of the people of South Africa. The purposeful leadership he gave in revitalizing the liberation struggle prompted Miriam Makeba, the South African Queen of songs and the globally acclaimed 'Mama Africa' to sing in his honor for paying the ultimate price for true leadership and friendship with the people of South Africa.

The liberation struggle became the yardstick to measure the Africanist outlook of Nigerian foreign policy with so much momentum that when the SOWETO uprising happened in 1976 and the outrage that followed the massacre of over 700 students expressing their rights to demonstrate against the apartheid regime in South Africa. The Nigerian government and its people redoubled their efforts and pressure on the international community to declare the white minority government in Pretoria a gangster regime and an illegal occupier that is perpetrating crime against humanity. Coupled with that, Nigeria provided succor to the victims of the uprising, sponsoring many of them to schools in Nigeria and elsewhere by providing scholarships. Nigeria even accommodated Tebeho Mashinini who was believed to be the leader of the SOWETO uprising so that he could continue with his education and stay far away from harm and target of the white minority government in South Africa.

The move by Nigeria to estrange itself from erstwhile friends who are perceived to stand against the interest of South Africans and the decolonization of Africa, and the show of support to the liberation struggle was at a time that no country in Africa dare to flex a muscle of bravado against United States of America and the United Kingdom. Not even powerful communist countries that command large political cloud in Asia and Latin America could do so. The courage exhibited by Nigeria to breath down the necks of the two most powerful countries in the western hemisphere and to come up with several policies and actions that compelled these countries to recant their support for the white minority regime in Pretoria and other bold moves at nationalization of British companies operating in Nigeria, shifted the global narrative of the liberation struggle to paying closer attention on African players against apartheid and the influence they suddenly and progressively wield.

Even the Soviet Union was astonished at the dauntless stand of Nigeria against apartheid and the confrontation it was having with sympathizers of apartheid worldwide. Many international observers and even the white minority government in Pretoria were not in doubt that Nigeria along with other African countries have indeed emerged in determining the direction of its destiny in international relations, in line with what affects the region directly or indirectly. Africa has attained a sizeable amount of political maturity in this period to decide for itself the nature of its aspirations and how to achieve it, without any interference from foreign interest. Nigeria made sure that everything she did during the liberation struggle was first to benefit Africans before anyone else. The period of the liberation struggle revealed without contradiction the level of the Africanization influence that Nigeria inserted and commanded in regional and global affairs.

Nigeria came at loggerhead with powerful countries of the world on behalf of the oppressed people of South Africa. Nigeria insisted that apartheid was an aberration to human rights, international security and fundamental freedom. It was not difficult to immediately recognize Nigeria government as the arrow-head of the liberation struggle other than the people of South Africa themselves. This was done with enormous responsibility and maturity that showed tremendous diplomatic prowess and moral authority in lashing even the ethical consideration for standing against apartheid and those who tacitly or openly support it. To be more specific on the seriousness that Nigeria place in winning against apartheid, on 31 July 1979, Nigeria nationalized assets of British Petroleum (BP) in retaliation to the seeming support that the United Kingdom gave apartheid in South Africa. The nationalization of BP declared how far Nigeria was willing to go to defend the rights of the oppressed South Africans and show the rest of the world that in the event of any global issues or international trade, Nigeria would rather align its political and economic interest with African countries. This was a huge statement and morale booster that emboldened organizations like the ANC, PAC, SACP, COSATU, etc., who were at the frontline of the liberation struggle.

Nigeria pursued the fight against apartheid with all the gravity its intention could muster. Some observers even claimed that ending apartheid became the only national interest tabled in the execution of Nigeria foreign policy during the period. The nationalization policy taken by Nigerian government was a direct aspersion against apartheid. Barclays bank, BP and other multinational corporations operating or doing business with apartheid regimes in South Africa were either nationalized or threatened to go out of business. Nigeria did not dwell on empty rhetoric in warning any country supporting the apartheid government in South Africa to desist or risk losing rights to doing business with the bourgeoning Nigerian economy.

Such strategy proved effective to a large extent. It was at the instance of the nationalization policy that the UK government and their commercial interests once again knew that they had to dissociate themselves from the apartheid regime. The nationalization policy sent a strong message and begun a trend which ignited a gradual but obvious demise of any legitimacy that the white minority government in Pretoria had with their sympathizers in the western hemisphere. Nigeria had to make some hard choices in favor of the liberation struggle which in some cases, was at the detriment of Nigeria's economy and rapport in the comity of nations. But it was a sacrifice worth making. It was the seal of Africanism archetype in accomplishment.

The Africanist posture of Nigeria at many international issues in any global arena has revealed a moral and even spiritual angle to its responsibility when it comes to taking a position that involves any African state. This has manifested in its past and present foreign policy inclination. The South African question left no country and people in doubt of where Nigeria stood on the issue of apartheid, even when some countries were afraid to take a position against apartheid for economic or strategic reasons. Nigeria became a beacon of courage for other African countries to draw strength from in the fight against apartheid and the consequences that comes with it. Nigeria dared western powers who secretly supported apartheid but openly showed indifference on the evil and threat to human rights and international security that the apartheid regime in Pretoria posed on the people, without recourse to established international norms.

Nigeria's commitment to ending apartheid and her unrelenting diligence in supporting the liberation struggle was noticed by all. When it became obvious that Nigeria will not back down in defeating apartheid, other countries who had a stake in the saga had to turn to Nigeria for guarantees. Former British Prime Minister Margret Thatcher visited Nigeria twice in one week to seek Nigeria's approach on how to end apartheid and ensure a smooth transition from white minority regime that has been ruling Mzansi for more than half a century. In fact, Margret Thatcher came to specifically ask Nigeria as an undisputed driving force in the liberation struggle, to ascertain the sincerity of the apartheid government led by Peter Botha in handing over power to a black majority government. It was a responsibility that only Nigeria could provide, given her enormous human, material, geo-strategic intelligence network, and moral resources at its disposal.

Frontline States plus Nigeria

To make a remarkable impact in ending apartheid, the Front-Line States (FLS) and Nigeria became the most visible rallying point of the liberation struggle on the continent. The FLS and Nigeria gave the white minority government one of the most effective resistance in the history of the liberation struggle. There was a growing need during the liberation struggle to cooperate, collaborate and form alliances with powerful individuals, institutions and governments that could pull enormous weight on the pressure to undermine the infrastructure and system of apartheid in Africa. The idea behind forming the lexicon of the FLS was to create a coalition of African countries that initially share boundary, ethnicity, homogeneity, proximity and history with native South Africa. It grew to include almost all the countries in Southern Africa, except for Malawi at the time. The FLS were the most active countries that were in support of the liberation struggle apart from Nigeria and the people of South Africa themselves.

The FLS was another frontier where the war on apartheid was fought as aggressively as it was fought inside South Africa itself. In order to perpetrate the system of apartheid in South Africa, the white minority regime in Pretoria adopted a strategy to destabilize neighboring states. According to Joseph Hanlon (1986), "South Africa's white leadership has concluded that the best way to preserve minority rule is to fight the war outside South Africa-to open up a 'second front' in the neighboring states. The goal is nothing less than control of the neighbors. Pretoria intends to keep them in a thrall and thus to create a buffer against both the southward tide of majority rule and against international campaigns for sanctions".

The FLS were mainly newly independent countries, governed by black majority rule of indigenous leaders and mostly by an array of revolutionary leaders that sort total and uncompromising freedom for Africans under colonial bondage. These countries created an alliance to battle apartheid after they realized that they could not achieve self-determination in South Africa or support the liberation struggle from an individual country approach. There was an imperative of a collective strategy by the independent African countries neighboring South Africa to present a common policy against apartheid, even though implementation of the policy sometimes requires each country play its role towards the achievement of the overall objective.

The FLS include Mozambique, Botswana, Zambia, Lesotho, Eswatini (Swaziland) and later joined by Zimbabwe and Angola as they gain political freedom. Few among the FLS are landlocked and depend largely on South Africa for access to the ocean. These natural impediments would later become a weakness that the white minority regimes in South Africa will take advantage of in coercing the FLS during the liberation struggle. The white minority governments in Pretoria used a tripod strategy of combining military, economic and political actions in a mix that is usually called 'destabilization' (Joseph Hanlon; 1986:2) to compel the FLS to depend on South Africa unconditionally for its survival. One of the useful contributions of Nigeria to end apartheid was eliminating or reducing the devastating impact of threat that the white minority government in Pretoria had on the FLS in connection to the Co-prosperity structure which the apartheid regime in Pretoria exploits to keep the FLS under leash. The FLS however are also rich in natural resources and other endowment but have been impaired by such location because they need access to the ocean for shipping and other commercial activities and other economic considerations of which South Africa called the shots.

Over the period of time apartheid lasted, the FLS will host the ANC, PAC, SACP, and provide moral and comradeship support that the freedom fighters will find obliging. But some of these FLS were not entirely free as the interest and large economy of South Africa squashed their dream of becoming a truly independent entity to determine its development and shape its future. They were not even completely free to support the Africanist agenda. In Southern Africa region, South Africa being the only white minority government surrounded by newly independent black majority governments, and using its enormous economic dominance in the region, was engaged in sponsoring dissention and civil wars in some of the FLS through the destabilization strategy mentioned earlier. The idea was to create anarchy in individual FLS so that they may not have the resolute attention to pay on the liberation struggle or even have sympathies for the freedom fighters. The civil war in Angola and Mozambique was a classic example of how the white minority regime in Pretoria meddle in the internal affairs of some FLS, sponsoring insurgency in order to discourage the support that these states give to the liberation movement.

Therefore, to sustain the apartheid system in South Africa the white minority government in Pretoria was inimical to the natives of not only Mzansi, but also an anathema to countries of mainly black majority governments of the FLS. The FLS had their share of the evil apartheid represents. Pretoria made sure that the destabilization of the FLS is done in perpetuity. They sponsored anarchy within the FLS states consistently to discourage any single state or supra-nationality to focus on the liberation struggle. The instigation of internal strife and protracted civil wars believed to be prompted by the white minority government in Pretoria to perpetually cause instability in the FLS, forced the government of Mozambique to sign an agreement with Pretoria known as the *Nkomati Accord*, a situation which Pretoria arm twisted Mozambique through this accord, to stop allowing the use of its territory as a refuge and launching pad for the liberation struggle. The Nkomati Accord therefore coerced the Mozambican government to sign a non-aggression pact with South Africa, made the Mozambicans to expel all ANC members, military as well as ordinary refugees, and improve talks on economic support (Joseph Hanlon; 1986:105)

Sometimes, security forces in Pretoria are known to organize assassination of political leaders of countries that are staunchly supporting self-determination of native South Africans and killing members of the liberation struggle who are on exiles in other countries even outside the FLS. There were many speculations that points to Pretoria as responsible for the political assassinations of prominent leaders of countries and some figure head of the liberation struggle. The death of Samora Machel of Mozambique, Tebeho Mashinini in Guinea, Murtala Mohammed of Nigeria and even Olof Palmer of Sweden were directly or remotely linked to the liberation struggle against apartheid in South Africa. Many crisis that engulfed the FLS during apartheid were sponsored to simply destabilize the economies of the countries and destroy any infrastructure that could enable them resist or assist the liberation struggle from making the expected impact against apartheid.

But Nigeria became one of the major if not the most significant keystone on which the liberation struggle found momentum within Africa to counter the enormous resources and support the apartheid regime swayed across the region of Southern Africa. The weight Nigeria brought into the struggle swayed the narrative of helplessness that the FLS seem to suffer in their bid to support the fight for the end of apartheid at its root. It became clear to many on the continent and overseas, that Nigeria has become the 'new global hub of anti-apartheid movement'. The seriousness and multipronged role Nigeria played in the liberation struggle was so pronounced that it was granted an unofficial member status of the FLS. At meetings and decisions taken on the liberation struggle by either African countries, the international community or regional bloc, there has always been consideration Nigeria on the same level as the FLS.

Nevertheless, the proximity of the FLS accorded them the opportunity to provide immense support for the liberation movement to thrive, by using their countries as ground for accommodating exiles from South Africa, training and logistics of freedom fighters, transportation and launching pad for the liberation struggle. However, the economic dominance of South Africa in the southern African region reduced the impact that FLS have hoped to make in isolating and coercing South Africa to abandon apartheid. The FLS however, prepared and provided pivotal platform for engagement and dialogue between the white minority regimes and the liberation struggle.

Working with the FLS, Nigeria security and intelligence community used border towns surrounding South Africa and the social infrastructure available in those locations to communicate and send correspondence with the freedom fighters within South Africa. Where there were no such infrastructures, Nigeria created them. Nigeria recruited 'pigeons' to send and receive correspondence from South Africa. The Casinos, pubs and markets of towns in Zimbabwe, Mozambique and Namibia that share boundary with South Africa were used to pump and sustain the energy of the liberation struggle within South Africa.

One of the biggest handicaps of the FLS was that they were economically linked and rely heavily on South Africa. The momentum that they could have put forward to strike a huge blow and increase the campaign against apartheid wanes in the face of the FLS poorly trained and under- funded military, lack of financial muscle to pull considerable weight in the international arena, a deficit in diplomatic prowess, and internal strife. The gulf created by these handicaps necessitated the need for Nigeria to fill up the gap. Nigeria was considered a FLS even though it was not geographically close in proximity to southern Africa. The political and economic influence and impact of Nigeria was so visible during the liberation struggle that a notion was entrenched where Nigeria was considered as a non -official member. Several literatures of the liberation struggle always refer to the FLS and Nigeria. According to Gilbert Khadiagala, the political connotation of the FLS implied that active commitment against minority rule in southern Africa determined whether a country was a frontline state. As at the time the FLS were constrained by the dominant power emanating from Pretoria, it was to Nigeria many of them had to rely for strategy, counter balance and implementation of the liberation movement's objectives in their respective states.

Nigeria used its economic fortunes to mount a successful campaign against apartheid South Africa both within the continent and across the globe. In the first instance, Nigeria recognized the legitimate role of the FLS to dismantle the oppressive and callous regime of apartheid in South Africa, and also identified with the anarchy these FLS are experiencing as a result. What Nigeria did was to make sure it countered the campaign of anarchy orchestrated by apartheid South Africa in the FLS, from Zimbabwe, Angola and Mozambique. The success of such counter measures is written down in history books. As these FLS became more stable, their independence established, and their security boosted by the help of Nigeria, the move was to bring the plight of native South Africans to the global audience. Nigeria sustained a mounting pressure on western nations who are supporting the white minority government in Pretoria through raising global awareness on apartheid by sponsoring international conferences, encouraging student protests in major cities of the world, sanctions and isolating South Africa in international forums.

Nigeria confronted the apartheid regime from different diplomatic, political, cultural and security dimensions and created a buoyant strategy to which gave a major boost to the liberation struggle. There have been instances when Nigeria bore the cost in full or part to fund implementation of the FLS, counter the economic blockade instigated by South Africa and the destructions of infrastructures of FLS. Nigeria contributed a total of about US$61 billion to support the end of apartheid. The huge material and financial resources that the liberation movement needed to make impact was provided by Nigeria. Along with the finances were the moral and political leadership that Nigeria also provided in replacing the infrastructures that South Africa destroyed in some FLS, where the famous statement by the Nigerian minister of foreign affairs at the time, Professor Bolaji Akinyemi stated, 'that where they destroy, we rebuild', came to be widely quoted. The foreign minister emphasized that whatever the white minority governments of South Africa destroyed in the FLS, Nigeria will rebuild it. The economic standing of Nigeria in Africa which was deployed without reservation to end racial discrimination in South Africa was acknowledged by the FLS and eventually identified Nigeria as a FLS even though it was not geographically located in Southern Africa.

Multilateral and Back-Channel Diplomacy

Diplomatic strategies and maneuvers played a subtle but game changing impact to the liberation struggle in South Africa. Nigeria was among the countries in the world, but arguably the most significant in Africa that brought its diplomatic and political clout to bear in articulating the end of apartheid. Very little is said or acknowledged on the role of Nigeria as Chair of the UN Special Committee against Apartheid. Nigeria served the longest as Chair of the Special Committee than any other country since the creation of the Committee in 1962. Nigeria did a fantastic job in navigating diplomatic options of mounting enormous pressure to the apartheid regime from the international stage, while also deploying vast resources within the continent to support the liberation struggle.

Nigeria took advantage of the doctrine of multilateralism gaining traction in the international system, and with the growing influence of the UN in promoting collective security and protecting human rights, to yoke the moral call to end apartheid in South Africa as its national interest. Nigeria pushed for the creation of the UN Special Committee to provide a platform for an astute diplomatic maneuvering never before seen or done by an African country on such a global scale. Nigeria's diplomatic engagement was strategic and with so much panache that it earned the country several commendation and accolade across the globe.

On the South African question, Nigeria through diplomatic persuasion insisted that the authority of the UN charter must be respected and upheld especially by the permanent members of the

Security Council and other powerful members of trans-national corporations, whom have used their influence to encourage and embolden the apartheid regime in acquiring arms of modern warfare aggressively against the natives and FLS. Nigeria insisted that loyalty to the UN must be derived from it being able to make decision on special issues of international concern and have those decisions respected wholly by its members. This call by Nigeria resonated with other countries who were disturbed by the human right abuse inside South Africa and who also knew that the legitimacy of the UN is being called to question by Nigeria through a moral, political, economic and social prism. Nigeria continued to pursue this call aggressively, but within the ambit of international law and multilateral expediency.

The oil embargo by oil producing states placed on South Africa was a huge success in terms of adherence to Nigeria diplomatic cloud in sponsoring such embargo. Nigeria made certain that the provision of the embargo was followed through. Such embargoes and sanctions shook the Pretoria government to its core. Oil was an important part of the white minority regime economic development and being isolated by countries who should make this commodity available, made the regime to start acknowledging the seriousness of the friends of freedom against apartheid, which jolted them to the reality that end of apartheid system is nigh.

The civil war between 1967 and 1970 in Nigeria was the only period since independence that Nigeria was not at the front row of fighting along with others to liberate the people of South Africa. When the civil war ended, Nigeria came back into the liberation struggle with more strength and determination to uproot any form of racial domination against the majority of black people of South Africa in particular, and Southern Africa as a whole. The retinue of top diplomats that represented Nigeria at national, regional and international fora all displayed maximum exuberance in eradicating apartheid on two fronts-through direct and back-channel diplomacy. It would appear that all the diplomats in charge of making sure apartheid is defeated swore to ensure it happened without hindrance. Nigeria's diplomatic role transcended political, economic and professional spectrum, it was a spiritual task as well.

Between 1970 and late 1980s, Nigeria crisscrossed the four corners of the world to raise awareness, canvass support and engage government of countries that were indifferent to apartheid but whose support will be influential in fighting the menace, even to those who were totally ignorant of what was happening in South Africa at the time. Through diplomacy, Nigeria made sure that every government and citizen in every clime understood apartheid as a crime against humanity and a major threat to international peace, security and freedom. To allow apartheid flourish therefore, was a recipe to undermine multilateral agreements to which many members of the UN assented, and on which international norms and order are predicated.

All the chairpersons of the UN Special Committee from Nigeria after the civil war and foreign affairs ministers as well, passionately followed the same direction and path in resolutely plotting for the end of apartheid. From Edwin Ogebe Ogbu, Leslie O Harriman, Akporode Clark, Maitama Sule, Joe Garba and Ibrahim Gambari, all of whom chaired the Special Committee and the last of whom oversee the transition and handing over of power from a minority to a majority democratic government in 1994. Nigeria seized every diplomatic opportunity to dismantle apartheid. Many of these Nigerian diplomats were known to present a common front at the UN and other international engagements of an Africanization agenda in Nigeria's diplomacy, to which South Africa and the liberation struggle was never missing in their speeches and focus. Some people even wonder if Nigerian diplomats during such periods were representing Nigeria or South Africa. Ending apartheid in South Africa became Nigeria's national interest within its foreign policy emphasis.

The Nigerian diplomats distinguished themselves very well in discharging the responsibility of assisting the liberation struggle achieve its objective within available resources which in any case was almost a *carte blanche,* so long as they accelerate the end to the white minority government in Pretoria in collaboration with those who shared the same desire. Subject to their conflict styles and persona, Nigerian diplomats one after another steered the ship of the liberation struggle through what is akin to deep international waters, despite encumbrances during the odyssey against all the elements, but steadily to victory that berth in 1994 democratic elections for a new South Africa. Even the white supremacist networks across the world acknowledged the obsessive commitment of Nigeria in the fight for this last stronghold of white minority regime in post-colonial Africa.

It was an elaborate diplomatic ordinance that Nigeria instituted against apartheid and against all odds that brought many hitherto cynics who do not believe in the will and power of an African resolve in any issue, to get won over to the side of reason-the reason being that apartheid was no longer a system that should be tolerated in a multilateral system, by any individual or country that truly stands for universal freedom, human rights and collective security. Nigeria did not just exploit multilateral institutions as the only strategy to fight apartheid and refuel the liberation struggle at the international fora, it also used several back-channel diplomacies to win the attention required to send apartheid to oblivion.

Nigeria's robust engagement in the struggle for the dismantling of apartheid regime in South Africa was orchestrated under a strict focus on the foundation of its foreign policy. The proactive diplomatic engagement of Nigeria, working in collaboration with other African countries resulted in the creation of several pressure groups even outside the continent. Nigeria was privileged to be invited by student bodies, academic conferences and charitable organizations to speak for the marginalized and oppressed in South Africa. Nigerian commitment to the liberation struggle accorded her respect among international right groups. Little wonder that Nigeria headed the UN Special Committee for 30 years, longer than any other country in the world. Nigeria became unyielding in its quest to dismantle apartheid and ardent attention to galvanized international support resulting in boycott of South African products, embargoes, economic sanctions and other strands of sanctions which did not end until majority rule and democracy was established in 1994.

Under the UN Special Committee, just as Nigeria sponsored the resolutions for the isolation of South Africa and insisted on the many embargoes and sanctions the apartheid government had to face from the international community, Nigeria also sponsored the resolution to bring back South Africa into the comity of nations as a responsible stakeholder when democracy was won and a majority government was in place. It followed a very dogged diplomatic and political commandeering of the strategies to bring the apartheid government into an uncomfortable position that they had to give in to pressure, apparently made more burdensome by Nigeria.

In 1994 when majority government was established, Ibrahim Gambari was the Nigerian Permanent Representative at the UN and as the same time Chair of the Special Committee who supervised the restoration of South African full membership back into the UN. In fact, he was the only other African in the exclusive cubicle where Mandela and Thabo Mbeki were sworn in as President and Vice President of the Republic. This was done to the admiration of and attendance of a large retinue of African Heads of States and Governments, within the continent and beyond. It was a historic event and the presence of a Nigerian at the political pulpit and standing at the center of the exchange of power to a black majority government, even though the Head of State of Nigeria was sitting in the audience with other colleagues. This has symbolized the merit Nigeria invested in the restoration of human rights and dignity of South Africans to the very end.

In the past, there were instances when Nigeria had to get across to the freedom fighters inside South Africa during apartheid. The white minority regime had their eyes and ears everywhere in South Africa, the reach of the regime even goes far beyond their borders because they have stooges and informers scattered across the FLS. Nigeria had several successful encounters where they surmounted the iron wall built by apartheid to keep dissent and opposition of the regime at bay.

But Nigeria were relentless and got a way to engage the services of 'pigeons' who are capable of evading the curious eyes of apartheid security and communicate with the insiders in South Africa.

This became necessary instead of an open confrontation or war with apartheid South Africa which Nigeria was indisposed to for obvious reasons. Diplomatic ploys and sheer power of persuasion of various kind were instead adopted to first convince those countries whom were hitherto uninterested in the inequality, discrimination and inhuman conditions of native South Africans, and also to use non kinetic measures to bring down the last vista of colonial contraption in Africa's political past. The power of diplomacy was preferred by Nigeria in order to protect lives, avoid or reduce collateral damage, and show that Africans could use 'civilize' means to denounce injustice and fix its own problems.

Nonetheless, Nigeria's role in the liberation struggle was so multifaceted in content and character that it was open to many interpretations and narrative. As Nigeria insisted, the liberation struggle could be won by peaceful means and they assisted the freedom fighters to actualize such objective. In another twist, even when it was becoming clear that revolts, sanctions, isolation and recrimination alone wasn't persuading Pretoria to give up apartheid, Nigeria made sure it became a nifty diplomatic buffer to make sure that it avoids any open confrontation between the liberation struggle and the white minority government that could lead to a civil war. However, Nigeria had always maintained the stance that it was open to a military option and the use of force to ensure that Pretoria does not orchestrate a major violence against the people like they did in the 1960 Sharpeville massacre.

Nigeria used organizations like the AU (formerly OAU) and other supra national bodies and lobby groups available to adopt and invoke the essence of their existence to fight what should not be allowed to exist. Nigeria used global sports festivals like the Olympic and Commonwealth games to push for outlawing the apartheid government in South Africa. Apart from several resolutions sponsored by Nigeria, there were boycotts, sanctions and defiance that were done globally at the instance of Nigeria in order to make the white minority government in Pretoria uncomfortable and unsustainable. The FLS made so much impact with the support of Nigeria in which they were provided with needed financial and moral backing to confront apartheid in their backyards and weed it out in whichever way their recommendation could get the Nigeria's buy-in. Nigeria understood the implication of regional cooperation as well as the multilateral nature of the international system and why such arrangements subsist.

The idea was to sustain a coordinated pressure from within Africa and internationally, for the diplomatic isolation of the white minority governments in Pretoria to give up its discriminatory policy of racial privileges to a minority group against the majority indigenous people who have no formal voice and broad-base legitimacy to overthrow the organized colonial arrangement that diminishes them, and of which they have no part in. Nigeria made sure that from outside South Africa, was an onslaught of diplomatic offensive directed at Pretoria to open up the space for a non-racial democracy and a back-channel pressure from a relentless citizen whose voices of anguish against apartheid are amplified by Nigeria's position in the UN Special Committee, its economic fortunes within the continent, and a determined people who would not rest until every black nation in Africa is free from political subjugation in the motherland.

A good example of Nigeria's diplomatic prowess was in hosting the first world Conference for Action against Apartheid, which was a follow up to Resolution 31/6 of the United Nations General Assembly (UNGA). In the resolution, UNGA had in their wisdom suggested that the conference be hosted 'in a country that was irrevocably committed to the eradication of this heinous crime against humanity'. There was no country ready at that material time with total commitment, seriousness and capacity like Nigeria. Nigeria dedication displayed at the UN by its collection of diplomats with the obsessive desire to eliminate the fathom of injustice that apartheid represent in Africa made the UNGA to formerly ask Nigeria to host the world conference.

The choice of Nigeria was also deliberate because hosting a successful conference of such magnitude will require a lot of financial resources and even though the world at that period was experiencing global recession, Nigeria was ready to make any financial commitment for the world to assemble and discuss the evil of a political arrangement that has befallen the black race in their own continent. This has made Nigeria arguably the only African country that took uncountable diplomatic shuttles from Lagos, New York, Oslo, and to any other country and region that needed to be represented in the conference, as well as take the message of the liberation struggle along with them on behalf of the people of South Africa.

Solidarity conference on Southern Africa held in New York in October 1981 was attended by Nigeria highest diplomatic entourage and in their capacity as the Chair of the UN Special Committee.

Nigeria participated in other seminars on US policy towards South Africa and have used such to declare its position on the issues of apartheid and also raise public awareness and support for the struggle. Nigeria mounted enormous pressure on USA to take a stand against the 'immoral, discredited and doomed system of apartheid or risk a political and economic isolation by the rest of Africa going into the future. Nigeria was able to mobilize governments who respects the tenets of decency and universal freedom, men and women of good conscience all over the world to support the struggle for self-determination of majority of the people in South Africa.

No country in Africa ever made such commitment in cash and in kind to the liberation struggle from the beginning to the end like Nigeria. Nigeria acceptance to unilaterally sponsor a very large number of government officials from several countries, diplomats, civil society organizations and anti-apartheid champions to the conference, who may not have attended due to the expensive cost of travel and other logistics into Lagos for the international conference against apartheid was resounding. The conference was generously attended by people and organizations from the four corners of the earth.

The Prime Ministers of some Nordic countries were very important personalities that physically attended the conference. Prominent among them was Olof Palmer, first as an opposition politician during the conference and later the Prime minister of Sweden. Olof Palmer worked closely with Nigeria to defeat apartheid in South Africa and of which rumor has it that he, just like Murtala Muhammed, paid the ultimate price for it. He was assassinated in the presence of his wife in downtown Stockholm while walking home from a night at the cinema. South Africa was rumored to have conspired to take him out due to his popular stand against apartheid. The complicity of the apartheid regime in South Africa in this assassination was never proven. Incidentally, Olof Palmer won the elections to become the Prime Minister of Sweden while he was attending the international conference against apartheid in Lagos. That omen created a good working relationship between Nigeria and Sweden that made significant impact on the liberation struggle.

Also, the attendance and gesture of having Heads of Governments and others whom will eventually take the mantle of their country's leadership, very important global players as well as internationally respected intellectuals and scholars, brightened the conference and beamed a spotlight and awareness of the evil of apartheid to a global audience. Some of the outcome of the conference produced an endearing campaign against military and nuclear collaboration with South Africa. It also recommended an arm embargo on South Africa. Also, the conference placed an immense pressure on world leaders and countries doing business with South Africa to reconsider their investments. Significantly, the conference while exposing the racial vices in South Africa, attracted the UN Resolution 421, which declared apartheid as a threat to international peace and security. Nigeria initiated or was at the crux of all this momentum.

Nigeria ran one of the most articulate diplomatic networks as far as the liberation struggle was concerned. The government of Nigeria realized early enough that to achieve considerable result against apartheid, a synergy of all its policies and collaboration with every international institution, group or countries with similar objectives was necessary. Nigeria was influential directly as a country in the creation of the UNSCAA, and brought its weight to bear on the promotion of the rights and access of native South Africans to education, social justice and racial equality, development and peace. They achieved this feat by networking with the IUEF, the Nordic countries, Negro groups in the US, Middle East States, OAU now AU, the Frontline States and other friends of freedom.

Fellowship of Brotherhood

As for Nigeria, apartheid was an embarrassment to the black race. Even more disheartening was the fact that this system of oppression and dehumanization was being perpetrated by foreigners on Africans in their ancestral land. It was a situation any proud African will resist, have to resist, and support its abolition. Such was the case resonating during apartheid and of which many Africans in the continent and in the diaspora saw the need to cooperate and rid Southern Africa in general from subjugation in the hands of non-Africans.

Nigeria already built a foundation which was solidly anchored on an Africanist world view to which her foreign policy is laid. Africa as the center-piece of Nigeria foreign policy made it easier to form a bond with the struggles and aspirations of many African countries because as far as Nigeria was concerned, no African is free until every African enjoys at least political freedom. Oppression of Africans anywhere is a slap on the faces of every African that thinks he or she is free. But to realize the dream of freedom for Africans that are still under the shackles of oppression and subjugation, there has to be a unity of purpose, cooperation and alliances between the broad spectrum of African leadership, followership and systems. This can come through a conscious and deliberate amputation of collective ignorance and a rethink of our colonial past. As Thomas Sankara would say to every African, 'we must dare to invent the future'.

Nigeria became the forerunner in building alliances with the FLS and other friends of freedom, as a strategic objective to ensure success of the liberation struggle. The enormous resources Nigeria wields in the 1970s, 1980s and 1990s helped to have its way with group that played a crucial role in the anti-apartheid movement in a nutshell. Nigeria saw the plight of majority of the oppressed South Africans as its own problem. As a region with shared dreams, aspirations and destinies, Nigeria built a robust comradeship with all members in the liberation struggle like the ANC, PAC, SACP, and have supported each of the strategies proffered by these groups, so long as it moves in the direction of success for the anti-apartheid movements.

Organization like the ANC that came into existence even before apartheid was formally instituted to fight inequality, subjugation and injustice, have had to collaborate with Nigeria to achieve its long-term objective of mass freedom. The relations and friendship shared between Nigeria and ANC was a rewarding partnership that culminated into ANC's victory and control of state apparatus in 1994. Although the friendship has experienced some challenges in the lifespan of the liberation struggle, but the camaraderie became established between these two entities and was elevated into a sort of brotherhood supplement.

The brotherhood alliance became more significant when several South Africans had to flee their country due to the clampdown of the apartheid regime on voices of dissent. Nigeria gave official passports to countless South Africans to enable them live and study in Nigeria and elsewhere. There were notable leaders and courageous personae of the liberation struggles that had to escape, arrest and imprisonment in South Africa that went on exile to Nigeria. Some have had to visit Nigeria to recharge and keep the furnace of the liberation struggle burning. For example, HE Thabo Mbeki was in Nigeria for seven years from 1979 to 1984 as the ANC representative in the country and indeed West Africa. Nigeria took care of him as their own.

Tebeho Mashinini, the famous teenager who led the Soweto uprising was also given asylum in Nigeria, when his safety was threatened by the apartheid government. Mashinini was encouraged by the Nigerian government to continue his education in Nigeria, but he declined and instead wanted to be given arms and ammunition to go back to South Africa and fight to chase out the white minority government. As brilliant and restless as his youthful energy could carry, Tebeho Mashinini later left Nigeria for Guinea where he was eventually assassinated. That could not have happened if he stayed back in Nigeria. The safety and security of more than 300 South Africans who were officially given passports by the Nigerian government and others not listed who came to Nigeria by fleeing the coup in Ghana that ousted Nkrumah were guaranteed safety and accommodation and most of them got quality education, many of whom became part of the new majority government formed in 1994 under democracy in South Africa. The contribution of Nigeria to the liberation struggle was a fight of brothers against a common foe. And this solidarity and friendship paid off.

It is instructive to mention that Mashinini could not understand why the version of the liberation struggle of South Africa had to be peaceful when the natives of other countries like Zimbabwe, Mozambique, Angola and even Namibia had to resort to armed insurgency before they gained their independence or freedom. He insisted that there can never be true freedom for the natives of

Mzansi if the only option open to the liberation struggle is to negotiate on peaceful terms with the oppressor. There were also worries about the strategy the white minority regime in Pretoria kept initiating with the numerous groups fighting for freedom under the anti-apartheid movement where they speak about peaceful negotiation with the groups, but at the same time they were aggressively bellicose and war belligerent in conduct. So it was Tebeho Mashinini's wish to be allowed to carry arms and he consistently expressed the view that the freedom South Africa needs can't be negotiated peacefully, that armed resistance was his most preferred approach to oust apartheid. Whether he was right or wrong, his assassination in Guinea could not afford him the latitude to understand or accept the fate of what has become of his beloved country after apartheid was squashed.

If history is anything to go buy, the role Nigerian played up to the twilight of democracy in South Africa depicts a trusted ally to the natives of South Africa and many leaders of conscience. For instance, Nigeria did not only stand by the people of South Africa and by extension the liberation struggle by mere rhetoric, but deployed tremendous amount of financial resources to push ahead the agenda of the liberation movement. Nigeria made strong financial resources available to the ANC during the campaign for the general elections which for the first time, the natives are allowed to vote. There were also instances when Mandela reached out to Sani Abacha, the Head of State at the time in Nigeria during the preparation for the inauguration of his presidency for financial assistance when funds seemed to be inaccessible from the apartheid government to conduct a transition ceremony. Nigeria obliged instantly. Perhaps the white minority government wanted to embarrass the ANC by starving the transition process of funds. Nigeria through General Sani Abacha sent $10 million to Mandela to cover the expenses of the inauguration ceremony. The funds were presented to Mandela by the first High Commissioner of Nigeria to South Africa.

The facts of Nigeria's financial contribution to various group actively in the vanguard of the liberation struggle was never in doubt. Even way before 1994, Nigeria made several undisclosed donations to the ANC. In 1984, the government of Nigeria sent a jet to Lusaka to meet with the leaders of ANC in its operational headquarters in Zambia. In that flight was the Nigeria's foreign minister and USD One million which he handed to OR Tambo on behalf of the government and people of Nigeria. The money was to assist the ANC in logistics and other operational cost and to boost the morale of the movement. OR Tambo was so excited that he asked the Nigerian Minister of Foreign Affairs who handed him the money to make a press statement to announce such generosity, but the Minister declined. OR Tambo was surprised by this generous yet surreptitious offer that he became heavy with emotions and almost immediately the excitement turned into a mix of intense gratitude as he thanked the minister with a stud handshake and teary eyes. Nigeria arguably contributed billions in dollars to the liberation struggle, some of which were done in secret due to the circumstances of the time, and other offers were done through regional organizations.

For Nigeria, supporting the liberation struggle in South Africa was a moral call and a just action and such was the steadfastness of every government that came to power since Nigerian independence. Many statements from the political leadership in Nigeria on apartheid suggested that there was no price or sacrifices too much to make for our brothers down south in the struggle against apartheid. Nigeria had supported and has continued to support native South Africans with material, moral and financial resources available at its disposal, to fight the just war of overthrowing the racist and murderous government of apartheid. In fact, Nigeria and its effort in ending apartheid is by far the most significant of a single African country in the history of the liberation struggle.

Major General Joe Garba (rtd), who spent a great deal of his professional appointment as Nigeria Foreign Minister, Chair of the UN Special Committee against Apartheid, and president of the UNGA in the past, revealed that there was no other issue that preoccupied the foreign policy of Nigeria after its independence like the South African question. In order to ensure Nigeria shows its determination to end any manifestation of foreign domination in South Africa, Nigeria has made friends with countries with whom she has nothing in common; she has conversely made enemies of erstwhile friends-all on account of their attitude towards the South African question. Nigeria's support to the liberation struggle also made her to formulate economic policies that have been detrimental to her own development because of our commitment to the eradication of apartheid.

PART 4: GREEN LAND AND DISTANT RAINBOW

Maitama Sule of Nigeria presenting anti-apartheid poster to the UN Secretary General

Consider all Options for Freedom in South Africa

'The generation that followed did not have the same concerns, none of its members attempted to follow the example of the past generation'

Cheikh Anta Diop

The nationalization policy of Nigeria in the late 1970s was directly linked to the liberation struggle. Many multi-national corporations doing business in Nigeria, most of them from rich western nations who tacitly supported apartheid by words, deeds or silence were nationalized by the Nigerian government. Very few companies escaped this orchestration as it became a veritable strategy to fight apartheid. For Phyllis Johnson and David Martin (1987), it was in this context that, for the first time, the major multinational corporations have been forced into agonizing reassessment of the value of their interest in South Africa and making a choice as to whether they will continue the risk of remaining committed to the apartheid system (pp. 315-316)

From the 1970s and into the future, Nigeria had sustained a vibrant political pressure pragmatic enough to prevail on western countries sympathetic to apartheid and use its influence to discourage the evil system. For the three decades Nigeria sat as the Chair of the UN Special Committee against Apartheid, it provided relentless leadership to ending apartheid in South Africa with gusto. Nigeria sponsored UN resolutions, lobbied pressure groups and sponsored international conferences, all in the bit to fight apartheid from every angle. Any challenge that Nigeria encountered during this period seemingly increased its resolve to end this crime against humanity and install a majority government that represents the interest of the majority. Political and diplomatic support of Nigeria to the liberation struggles has been greatly acknowledged by Nordic countries and others who *contributed in the struggle for the eradication of the oppressive apartheid system from the continent.*

Nigeria was also specially recognized in the entire calculation of the liberation struggle due to its rising power in Africa. In 1986, Olusegun Obasanjo was selected among other prominent global leaders, known as the Commonwealth Eminent Persons Group, to visit Nelson Mandela in prison as start-up of process that would lead to his eventual release from Robben Island. While the selection was to recognize the role of Nigeria in the anti-apartheid era, it also symbolized the leadership position of Nigeria within the context that such struggle was fought and how Nigeria reinvigorated and ensured a revolutionary regime change in South Africa.

Nigeria from inception, was ruled along capitalist free market economy direction, with its tendencies and shortcomings. Successive Nigerian governments from independence and especially after the civil war, were so aligned. However, in the 1970s, 80s and part of 1990s, the Nigerian academia, Trade Unions, Civil Servants and student bodies had become actively involved in lending their voices to developments in the country including attempting to influence government direction in global developments. Many of them have become strongly influenced by socialist maxim. The contribution of Nigerian citizens was so deliberate that they influenced successive Nigeria government policies on apartheid. The Nigerian civil society organizations in these periods pushed for a vibrant engagement against apartheid in Africa and South Africa in particular. There were also more than hundred active demonstrations and protest by Nigerian students in tertiary institutions across the country against apartheid.

Despite the central role of ideology in playing a part in the anti-apartheid movement, the apartheid system could not have been overrun with just deep-thinking rhetoric. Nigeria came in to play what is arguably the most pragmatic and progressive role in winning on the side of the liberation and provided the substance needed to turn ideas into workable reality and sustain the fight to liberate every nook and cranny of the continent from any trace of political subjugation and colonialism of any guise. Nigeria was instrumental in the setting up ideologically charged debates in schools and in the halls of regional organizations, due to its positions on Africa to which many have to study and understand the driving notion to Nigeria's leadership style in Africa. It is not a coincidence therefore that the Nigerian position on continental issues sometimes appear to create a divide between socialist and capitalist lining. Every Nigerian position is however done in the interest of Africa.

Therefore, Nigeria wasted no time in exploiting the opportunity of its standing with the USA to remind them of their responsibility to international peace and security. Nigeria has always insisted that if the USA will not intervene and bring its support to bear at stopping apartheid, the world and Africa in particular will descend into armed conflict and anarchy. Nigeria did not mince words in showing that they are willing to encourage the resort to full scale arms struggle in the effort to defeat apartheid, including support for armed insurgencies in particular, in alliance with the frontline states. The threat for a full arm insurrection by the majority people of South Africa was apparent and indicated a chaos that loomed in the entire region.

It was explicitly clear that although Nigeria considered a negotiated peaceful approach towards the dismantling of apartheid as the best approach, it could also support a full scale armed struggle. It was the estimation of Nigeria that if apartheid was not totally dismantled, it could lead to the destabilization of the entire region. Nigeria was therefore ready to support the activities of the freedom fighters, including whatever tactics, be it political, economic, and cultural or armed resistance that they decide to deploy to end it. Nigeria was fully conscious of the fact that the freedom fighters in the liberation struggle will need tremendous assistance to make impact that could be considered widespread enough to undermine apartheid.

To undermine apartheid within South Africa was however slow, but progressively surely, and that was because the freedom fighters in South Africa did not have the political power to determine their own power trajectory, development, political and economic system. Nigeria tried as much to fill that political void and add to the volume of the political voices of the oppressed black people of South Africa in the international community. As a country who have 'organized the largest and most representative conference ever to meet on the issue of apartheid' and acknowledged by OR Tambo to be a country that believed in action, Nigeria beamed the light against apartheid with an obsession of a bee to a hive and have arranged many significant platforms that revealed unmistakably, Nigeria's commitment to the liberation struggle. For Nigeria, ending apartheid was by any means necessary and it is nothing short of a task that must be done, in whichever way possible.

There is no National Interest

In 1976, Nigeria established the Southern Africa Relief Fund (SARF) in order to provide funding for a holistic and comprehensive support in political, economic and social sphere of the liberation struggle. The purpose of the fund was also to provide relief materials and other assistance to the South African victims of apartheid regime, including educational assistance and the promotion of general welfare. Under the government of General Olusegun Obasanjo, then as military ruler, the government made a contribution of US$3.5 Million to the fund. Obasanjo himself made a personal contribution of US$3,000 while members of the Supreme Military Council made a contribution of US$1,500 each. In addition, the Nigerian Public sector and its civil service also contributed 2% of their monthly salary every month to the Fund. The intelligentsia and university students across Nigeria had to skip lunch each day for six months and the cost of the meal added to the Fund. The SAFR at the time was known as the "Mandela Tax" in Nigeria.

The financial contributions of various Nigerian governments to the liberation struggles have been relentless and consistent. The ANC as an organization have received large sums of money from Nigeria, the tune of which many other African countries could not afford to part with, for the simple reason that they could not afford it or did not have the fervent commitment of Nigeria to the liberation struggle. The monetary contributions of the Obasanjo's government alone, from 13 February 1976 to 30 September 1979 was put at twenty million pounds. This amount was even admitted by no other than former president Thabo Mbeki himself in an occasion of Nigerians in Diaspora living in South Africa, in honor of former Olusegun Obasanjo on 25 May 2012 (Nigerian Voice Newspaper: 2013). Every successive government in Nigeria gave the ANC large but sometime unspecified amount of money in foreign currencies openly, but many times through covert financial support. Some of these financial assistances have been mentioned.

Nigeria has invested so much capital in human, strategy, logistics and financial assets to free South Africa from the shackles of apartheid. A large number of people across the continent of Africa knew about Nigeria's role in the liberation struggle, some knew through tales, others through books and school education. Within Nigeria, post-apartheid South Africa jolted many social scientists to interrogate the rationale of Nigeria foreign policy thrust and what benefits to expect from the humanitarian nature of such foreign policy in Africa. Current reality of Nigeria and South Africa relations shows that Nigeria's foreign policy and its national interest does not reflect the nature of interactions.

The fact remains that Nigeria may never recover from South Africa what it invested to defeat apartheid. For what it is worth, Nigeria was more preoccupied with pushing forward the African *centered foreign policy* of which the motive was to liberate the black race anywhere, especially in the motherland, than any other expectation-whether personal or public. It would be argued further that since the preoccupation of the liberation struggle from the Nigerian perspective was *the defeat of* apartheid, the aftermath shows that the quality of interaction and integration between the people of Nigeria and South Africa did not grow as a result of the liberation struggle, as there were few interactions among the people of both countries during such period. Political interactions between the governments of these countries became the norm, instead of engendering people to people integration.

As it is currently experienced in South Africa, people of African descent are positioned at the lowest rung of the food-chain. This is borne out of the fact that the ANC government does not have the political will, and many immigrants as well as the native majority are not adequately educated to reconstruct the system to better redistribute land and other factors of production that will give advantage to blacks in South Africa. Little wonder that the informal sector in *Mzansi* is dominated by immigrants of African origin, most notably Nigerians. Some of the educated Nigerian migrants are restricted from engaging in the formal sector of the economy which is still dominated by the minority white South Africans and a small collection of natives some of whom received training and education in Nigeria.

Until recently, there were no Nigerian banks operating in South Africa, despite the large number of Nigerians living and doing business in South Africa. Apart from the informal sectors, Nigerians are restricted through various diplomatic and political channels from making a foot print in the formal sector of the economy. This is to avoid any meaningful competition that could give Nigerians or immigrants an edge in the polity. From the social angle also, there is no one in doubt about the love-hate relationship that has escorted interactions between the people of Nigeria and South Africa in recent times. Although the love-hate relationship cannot be blamed on ignorance alone, but quite frankly, it came from the bad behavior of some Nigerians living in South Africa. There are so many instances of such.

Away from the above, hopefully, rapid educational opportunity for native South Africans will eventually bridge the gap and gradually open more space for the natives and African immigrants to be involved in the formal sector. Joe Garba, a Nigerian military officer and diplomat who played a significant role in synergizing Nigeria's contributions to the liberation struggle under the period in focus, has agreed to this suggestion. Therefore, education for the natives might not only increase their value in Mzansi but also improve social, cultural and economic relations with others. Through education, the people of Mzansi will read, hear and understand the sacrifices made on their behalf and accept the complexity within the environment, convolution and inevitability of some actions taken by Nigeria just to ensure the success of the liberation struggle.

Many African countries including the people of South Africa have blamed Nigeria for its pro-west posture against popular African position in continental leadership and ideological persuasions. What many of these countries and critics may not have noticed was that the pro-western inclination ascribed to Nigeria in post-independence was nothing compared to the mentality of its citizens across extents. Nigeria official positions often appear pro-west, but it is deeply Africanist. Nigerian citizens during the liberation struggle were radical and critical of western approach, particularly as it revealed the capitalist misdemeanour of the political elite. The academia,-civil servants and student bodies and even the informal sectors, had awaken the consciousness of the nation towards African socialism that would arm twist the political class to pay special attention to the spirit behind the liberation struggle. This was quite instructive because in the overall goal of ending apartheid, the apartheid system itself almost distracted some friends of freedom from the objective of the liberation struggle.

Nothing else mattered to Nigeria more than insisting that Africa is free from political subjugation and supremacy by foreign elements. Nigeria invested all its financial and human energy to make sure that not only Zimbabwe, Angola, Namibia was rid of white minority rule, but that South Africa, the stronghold and intellectual capital of apartheid must come crashing down. But instead of receiving accolade and commendation, there is nothing about what Nigeria assisted to achieve in South Africa. No Street or public building named after any Nigerian that may have facilitated a robust support to the liberation movement in South Africa. Except for maybe Fela Anikulapo-Kuti and Chinua Achebe who were named after some university halls in Gauteng province, and that was done on their individual merit to Arts and literature generally. No names of Nigerians linked to the liberation struggle exist in the streets or public building of South Africa.

Just take a walk into the Union building in South Africa that serves as the official seat of government and walk into the 'freedom park' hall where there is a huge mural of black history, of black people across the world and particularly in Africa who made heroic and significant impact to black struggle and the dignity of the black race in Africa; there is no single picture of a Nigerian in that collage. To anyone that observe this obvious anomaly, the response is always that they are not aware of the contribution of any Nigerian to fit into this collection. Now the 'freedom park' is a national monument that attracts visitors across the world any time in South Africa. It is a very pronounced tourist destination for foreigners and also young and old citizens of Mzansi.

The success of Nigeria in bringing apartheid to an end came with a significant cost to the country and its people. Interestingly, it will later be a reality that the enormous resources (both human and material) Nigeria pulled to end the evil system of apartheid directly or indirectly earned her a loathsome persona from the people of South Africa. Either way, the despicable behavior and attitude of South Africans towards Nigerians and vice versa is imminently embarrassing to the memory and goodwill of the liberation struggle. It could only make sense when we remember the impact of the apartheid system on the victims.

However, it has been reflected that the liberation struggle built a sense of purpose and confidence in Nigeria and its people about themselves. While the assertiveness of Nigerians played a great part in the liberation struggle and disrupting apartheid, such character later became a challenge to inter communal interactions between Nigerian and South Africans in post-apartheid era. There are many South Africans who admitted that even though they don't know much about what Nigeria did in South Africa during apartheid, they are assured of the fact that Nigerians are the only class of the black race that could stand up to the white man. Whatever has given them that impression cannot be unrelated to some perceived character traits that Nigerians possess.

The ostentatious lifestyle, assertive character and sometimes disorderly and corky nature of Nigerians will later create grievances and intolerance by native South Africans who are still reeled under the impact of apartheid on their psyche. Apartheid created in the natives a bunch of people with a victim syndrome, obscured sense of self-esteem and a distorted identity that affects how they relate with visitors or anyone they consider a stranger. This perception has permeated politics, economy and social sphere of intra and inter communal relations of the natives and other Africans. As a result of such mismanaged perceptions, there became a deficit of trust, love, confidence, harmony and transformative socialization to meet contemporary people's exchanges in Africa.

The history of Nigeria's contribution in ending apartheid could not solve the widely contradictory relations between the people of both countries. Some refer to Nigeria /South Africa relationship as a love-hate relations. This situation is principally due to the underutilization of historical bonds that should have been exploited from a socio-cultural as well as political economy angle by the leadership of these countries. Many people interviewed in South Africa have expressed different reason why they think the relationship between citizens of these two great countries aren't cordial.

Some of the reasons are plausible while some are just out rightly laughable. Consider a group of young South Africans who think that they have every reason to distrust Nigerians because 'even the white man does not trust a Nigerian'. Others have insisted that Nigerians have an attitude problem that makes them too ostentatious and megalomaniac who want to dominate every space they find themselves, even in another man's country. Nigerians are lawless, others have opined. 'My problem with them is that they befriend our sisters and later convert them into prostitutes or even something worse'.

There is hardly any reason provided by the people of Mzansi over their issues with Nigerians that cannot be verified. It was the interview with Ma' Mathlou, who has been married with children to a Nigerian and have lived and schooled in Nigeria during the liberation struggles that gave her outlook to why the story of the struggle from the Nigerian perspective is blurred to South Africans. She summarized it to be a relationship that has not be tested to the young generation of South Africans to appreciate. These young South Africans, many of whom know about Nigeria only through what they see on Nollywood (Nigerian movies), and cannot reconcile it with the level of community poverty that they see in the movies, with the affluence that Nigerians in South Africa display, sometimes gotten through dubious and diabolic means.

The wealth displayed by Nigerians in South Africa and the shenanigan of some Nigerians have exposed both South Africans and Nigerians to danger, and have reduced the camaraderie that has been forged by their ancestors during the liberation struggle that should have spilled into post-apartheid relations between the two countries. But alas, what the young generation of both countries experience in an unhealthy competition and even animus.

To put it discernibly, Nigeria and South Africa relations post-apartheid is squarely focused on government-to-government interactions and little of every other sector. Any African progressive would be happy with the political cooperation between the two countries that birth the ideas and eventual formulation of the New Partnership for Africa Development (NEPAD) and the Nigeria South Africa Biennial cooperation. The political leadership of Nigeria and South Africa at the time projected to its people the opportunities and vibrant future of what is possible if the two countries cooperate and interact more closely.

The cooperation between Nigeria and South Africa has borne fruits in various ways that the continent currently benefits. For instance, it was the cooperation between the two countries through their ratifications that transformed the OAU into the AU. 'Without the support of Nigeria and South Africa, and the skillful manner they handled the challenges thrown at the continent from certain quarters, the African Union would have been quite different from the one we have now and would stand less chance taking Africa forward'(Shinkaiye JK, 2002:12)

The collaboration however dwell more on the political sphere of things. Little investment was done on other sectors like cultural exchanges, historic documentaries and African socialization that could bring the people closer. During the liberation struggle, it was in Nigeria national interest to eradicate apartheid in South Africa, but that has changed when democracy was achieved. However, it currently appears that it is not even in South Africa national interest to make sure that Nigeria and its people feel secured within South Africa. To follow recent events over the past decades on Nigeria and South Africa, a sense of mutual suspicion among the people is the norm so much that it put to shame the efforts and alliance that the ancestors of both countries entered in the past to confront common challenges.

The manifestation of the socio-cultural immaturity and economic imbalance when it comes to inter communal relations between South Africa and Nigeria is easily understood in the issues around immigration, crime and injustice. African immigrants living in

South Africa regardless of whether they are Nigerians or not, are constantly in fear of molestation, intimidation and violence perpetrated by South Africans. The protracted xenophobic violence or what some prefer to call black on black violence is an aberration to the significant human and material resources deployed across Africa to free South Africans from the clutches of bondage. The many cases of attacks on Nigerian businesses and interests in South Africa speaks volume and can be a book on its own. But the Nigeria-South Africa collaboration have been sold short of what it should be.

South Africa is no longer viewed by many Africans as the regional powerhouse of Southern Africa in a positive way. Instead, the natives are viewed as people who cherish hate over love, have become a barbaric collective instead of humanity and togetherness. It would appear that the moment democracy and majority rule was achieved in 1994, the natives transferred the resentment of their long servitude during apartheid to other Africans.

After 1994, the orientation of the native South African became diluted and it also became obvious that they have adopted some unusual behavior inimical to African civilization. The communal tendency known with Africa disappeared when majority rule began. Native South Africans became individualist, secluded and occidental, in a region where the people are originally oriental. The difficulty for native South Africans to see themselves as Africans and integrate in the grand scheme of pan Africanism defeats the purpose of African development away from ideological, social and cultural dimensions which as stated earlier, was ignored and sacrificed on the table of political convenience.

The Nigeria South Africa relations is imbecilic. In the mind of the people, this relationship is not as good as the government of both countries want the world to believe. It is obvious that the people of Nigeria and South Africa do not really get along. This happenstance is beyond just some character traits or even the experience of citizens who were privileged to visit these countries. It is embedded in a perception crafted by the violence, tensions and betrayal that has come to typified Nigeria and South Africa interactions.

Resentment in Post-Apartheid South Africa

Post-independence political leadership in Africa has not been a very exciting story for many observers of regional development. The robust and visionary leadership of political leaders during independence brought so many changes in ideological, political and socio-economic direction for the continent. These leaders laid the foundation for a solid African perspective to governance and projected the African character in many sectors, including the African identity. Those who came after them in the 1970s, 1980s and 90s, were also builders of the African approach. However, the 21st century exposed lots of mistakes and misdirection of the African contemplation. The political misdemeanor of leaders that emerged during this period had a negative and profound impact on the socialization threshold of the people, whose rapport were manipulated to engender retrogression instead of progress, mutual suspicion of our collective drive instead of unity in Africanism.

The leadership deficit that Africa experienced some decades after independence, gradually became a major feature of individual and collective misfortune for numerous countries. Many countries were engulfed in civil wars, black on black violence, others destroyed by corrupt leaders, as yet majority became economically paralyzed. There was hardly any country in Sub Saharan Africa at the time that was doing well. Apart from political instability, economic prosperity was also lacking with the exception of South Africa. Just as many countries in the continent started well with so much promise whilst the people of South Africa were in bondage, such became the fate of those countries in Africa when South Africa became stable and a beacon of economic development and democracy in Sub Saharan Africa.

As the people of South Africa began to enjoy dividends of democracy after apartheid, the story of some African countries who fought along with native South Africans to attain majority rule became that of woe. Democratic and stable South Africa eventually was the attraction for economic migrants and asylum seekers from across Africa. The number of these migrants kept increasing in South Africa as the economic fortunes of the country swelled. This was happening at the same time as other African countries were sliding deeper into political and economic misery. Countless of these migrants were optimistic that the camaraderie struck during the liberation struggle with the leadership of democratic South Africa would provide some form of sanctuary or count for something. Alas, that became a pipe dream.

The history of xenophobia in South Africa became a malignant cancer at the foot of African unity and development. For the very reason why black on black violence persist in South Africa, the continent could not move forward in confidence due to the pains such cancer of disunity, self-hate, ignorance and lack of a deliberate effort for social cohesion for Africans by its government. The beacon of hope that stable and democratic South Africa represented for African migrants in that country quickly became hades. Lives and properties of fellow Africans are extinguished in a second, at the slightest provocation, because the culprit and the victim are not even aware that they are brothers (Mfowethu)

The stories of the liberation struggle like many aspects of African past, had not been talked about, celebrated or even archived. In cases where such history was recorded, it was hardly done by Africans themselves. As usual, this part of the story is often told by non-Africans, a situation that has misrepresented and made Africa one of the most misunderstood continents of the world. The most unfortunate of it all was the fact that leaders of the majority government in South Africa have also shied away from telling its people of the need to accommodate Africanism in their conduct with migrants on the grounds that majority government was achieved through a good neighbor approach embedded in our African mantle. It would appear that the ANC government deliberately muted that part of their history from the people. Granted, sometimes certain aspects of history are better not told, but that are often unpleasant ones. The contributions of some African countries whose citizens are now immigrants in South Africa cannot be an unpleasant part of history to hide. Rather, it should be able to show and speak of what Africans can achieve together with unity of purpose. It was a story of heroic deeds against foreign invasion of the motherland.

For the same reason that majority of South Africans do not know much about the history of apartheid from the African perspective, so is the embarrassing dementia portrayed by leaders across the continent on the vision of its founding fathers, of a united and prosperous Africa. The fragmentation of Africa and its people by Africans themselves has made the continent averse to an inclusive and sustainable development that is hinged on a political direction that can project the African as an indigene, regardless of which country he or she is born or resides.

If the political leadership of South Africa decided on the policy of silence over the contributions of other countries in the liberation struggle, surely, it will be the responsibility of historians or those who went on exile across the continent and returned when majority rule was achieved to ensure that the people never forget the relationship forged. Maybe if these actors in South Africa have taken the obligation to build a history around the friends of freedom and make its people recognize and have knowledge of the role other African states played in the liberation struggle, perhaps a sense of negritude will have been built and sustained in intra Africa socialization in South Africa and the continent in general. So far, many African countries are begrudged with South Africa over the treatment of its citizens without recourse to the friendship of years back.

South Africans are exposed to a selective narrative of history around the liberation movement, who or which country stood by them during that period of scorn. The knowledge of the liberation struggle was based on half-truths, misrepresentation of facts or deliberate silence about some actors who made the struggle a success. Misrepresentation of facts and deliberate silence did not just happen perchance, there were events and reasons why it was allowed to stay that way. Since the ANC government started ruling South Africa in 1994, it became obvious that muting the part of history that speak on the contribution of Nigeria in particular was strategy they were willing to adopt.

There are circumstantial motives on how and why the policy of silence and the precedence to achieve it was obvious. Schools in South Africa post-apartheid do not teach history, especially on the liberation movement. Previously, the country was shut out to the rest of the world and the apartheid regime control what information comes into public knowledge. This strategy was adopted by the ANC governments when it comes to the liberation struggle. Many citizens in that era, do not know what their kin who were on exile in other African countries were doing on their behalf. They only knew the 'soldiers' fighting within its borders and very few whose charisma and crusade on the liberation struggle were very vocal from outside.

Even the ANC political school that train and build capacity for the people of Mzansi and will transform them from freedom fighters to decent contributors to the political economy of South Africa, does not mention any contribution of the liberation struggle from Nigeria. According to a Nigerian known as Chief Iche Udeji Jonas, 'the ANC political school is a place where the history of South Africa, the history of the ANC, the contribution of most South African revolutionaries and some aspect of political science are taught to members of the ANC'. The ANC Political School is the best place to know about the contributions of the FLS, (which is part of the curriculum) and where they learn various accounts of the liberation struggles, but there is nothing whatsoever about what Nigeria brought to the struggle.

Another reason begets a deliberate attempt by the ANC to only acknowledge people or countries that they deem fit or of which gives them international appeal. Almost immediately after majority rule was established in South Africa with the help of Nigeria, Nigeria human rights record became tainted by military dictatorship, and South Africa was used to vilify Nigeria. South Africa suddenly became the bastion of democracy in Africa and such status brought the political leadership of Mzansi at loggerhead with Nigeria. Nelson Mandela wasted no time to color the military junta of Sani Abacha of Nigeria bad for obviously contravening some provisions of human rights norms. Nigeria leadership at that time felt betrayed by South

Africa for not considering the human rights imbroglio as a peculiar internal challenge towards the process of nation building.

Deliberately or by default however, Native South Africans have been exposed to celebrate those individuals and countries that makes the ANC government look good in the eyes of the people. The street of Mzansi is surfing with knowledge of the outstanding role played by Kwame Nkrumah of Ghana, Julius Nyerere of Tanzania and Muammar Gaddafi in supporting the liberation struggles, even more than the very significant role of people and countries of the FLS like Kenneth Kaunda of Zambia and Samora Machel of Mozambique. It was obvious that the leadership of Nkrumah and Nyerere influenced the liberation struggle a great deal. In addition of providing the liberation struggle with an abode to situate its operations in West and East Africa, the most significant support that captured the popularity of Ghana and Tanzania in the history of the struggle was the ideological direction it gave the movement.

Nkrumah, gave a philosophical narrative to which the people of Mzansi bought completely. His political thought resonated with building the African identity and by extension, the identity of the black race anywhere in the world. Many black nations outside Africa perceived Ghana as the cradle of African distinctiveness and reawakening due to the eloquence and vision of Nkrumah in his life time. At the core of the liberation struggle was a thirst for ideological doggedness which more than anything else, fuelled the fire that kept burning in the hearts of freedom fighters in South Africa.

The gap Ghana and Tanzania filled in exposing the ideological component of the liberation struggle may have endeared South Africans to remember Nkrumah and Nyerere more than any other actors who are worth the mention in anti-apartheid campaign on the continent. Besides, the period of the liberation struggle was more about the emancipation of the mind than just collecting back a nation from its usurper, and Nkrumah knew that during his days. After all, when the soul of a nation is troubled, the appreciation of a direction, power of words, or philosophy count more than material satisfaction.

Deliberately or not, the contributions of other countries and Nigeria in particular was silent. In fact, many South Africans have expressed disbelief to learn that Nigeria played any role at all in the liberation struggle. Some came up with various notions and argument of why they think Nigeria could not have played any role or even if it did, may not have been significant to make any historical imprint in the discourse of the liberation movement. It is therefore a big surprise for many Nigerians to learn that the efforts of its compatriots in the liberation struggle had been pushed into oblivion by people who should be witnesses.

History indicates that the organization that transformed to what is known today as the ANC, was a prolific tale of demand for human dignity and liberty. The ANC was seen as the traditional symbol of the liberation struggle in South Africa since apartheid regime was instituted. However, like any social construct typical of change, the agenda of the organization started changing to accommodate differences in opinion and ethics. Such changes also brought forward the necessity for its members or others to create similar organizations which they feel could best demonstrate how they want to achieve freedom. The existence of these organizations has come to influence how many acknowledge or disregard the contributions of the good intentions of other African countries in the liberation struggle.

Nigeria's role in the liberation struggle was first interned by the majority government of representative democracy in South Africa, and there were assumptions to understand why this policy of silence lingered. It may be due to the fact that Nigeria supported other protagonists of the liberation struggle like the PAC and SACP during the liberation struggle and the ANC saw this move as an affront to its leadership position in the liberation movement. The PAC and SACP were breakaway factions of the ANC for reasons that are political, ideological and operational. The ANC wanted to be seen as the lone face of the liberation movement. The internal wrangling between the ANC, PAC, SCP and other freedom fighters was not of any major concern to Nigeria, because Nigeria saw in each of them, actors in the same struggle. However, the ANC would later show its displeasure through a seeming governmental policy to *deliberately* ignore Nigeria's commendable role in the struggle.

Others thought that it will be illogical for Nigeria to support South Africa during the liberation struggle given its history. Nigeria has always been a free-market economy and capitalist in orientation. To them, Nigeria has never been a socialist state or founded on socialist ideologies and that shots contrary to the type of country that would support the liberation struggle, which by the way got its legitimacy, goodwill and temerity to fight against apartheid based on socialist mantra. They saw Nigeria as too friendly and strategic to western powers to even contemplate fighting against apartheid, a regime that was sustained by the same capitalist appetite. Many like them didn't know that the Nigerian state, its leadership and people were at that period hinged on socialist stimuli despite the capitalist oriented free economy disposition known by it. Indeed, Nigeria used its capitalist strength to destroy apartheid in Southern Africa.

Also, there were assumption that the ignorance about Nigeria's role in the liberation struggle could be a deliberate effort by the *minority white* (white minority dynamic) whom later formed the majority government with the ANC, to cleverly downplay Nigeria's role as pay back for the resources and force to which Nigeria brought in to topple the apartheid regime. They were never happy about it and they worked in the shadows to make sure that Nigeria and the ANC led majority government constitute more contradictions and unhealthy competition in the life of their relationship, where there should be a unity of purpose between Nigeria and South Africa.

The black-on-black violence that South Africa is infamous for is a direct effect of ejecting history and not knowing who their real friends are. The youth on whose shoulders rest the responsibility of building a future are ignorant or deliberately allowed to erase a fact of history from which the knowledge of building its future should require. It will be counter-productive if the people of South Africa are allowed to ride with the impression that they were alone in their dark moments of foreign oppression by a white minority population without the assistance of other Africans. As much as the Boers have transformed themselves from Europeans to Afrikaans, it is with serious pleasure that the natives do their utmost best to reinvent themselves into a cosmopolitan example of Africa with a sense of pride and direction that beam towards an African renaissance.

South Africa is a bastion of vibrant African history, rich in tradition and pragmatic in Pan-Africanism. Yet the country has chosen to exclude some part of its history from its story. Very few among its political and academic community actually speak for these stories to be heard. Miriam Makeba of blessed memory sang in honor of General Murtala Muhammed of Nigeria who gave the liberation struggle the energy to the eventual demise of apartheid. Even though this may not be loud enough, but it is very commendable. Interestingly, no Nigerian has been immortalized in South Africa by naming a street or public building after them. Anyone will notice this when they visit the Union Building and Freedom Park in Pretoria, South Africa.

As far as many were concerned, the radical foreign policy of Nigeria during the regime of General Murtala Muhammed and later Obasanjo and subsequent leadership that follow in Nigeria, pushed forward the era of African nationalism as the bases for ensuring victory for the liberation struggle. This resonated and gave momentum to the freedom fighters both within and outside South Africa to engage apartheid in a strategic African standpoint. This is a fact of history that can never be erased by silence, ploy or half-truth. The history of the liberation *struggle* can never be complete without the mention of Nigeria, not even a hardline critiques of Nigeria could deny this fact.

* * *

On a deeper reflection, there is also a palpable grudge by the natives of South Africa against the ruling ANC. The ANC have been in power since 1994, but could not translate such democracy into a promising future of hope and material benefits to the people. If some of the founding fathers and mothers of the liberation struggle were alive, they would certainly be ashamed of the leadership decline towards prosperity that the ANC government has exhibited after Mandela and some extent Thabo Mbeki's regimes. It will appear that the African leadership represented by the ANC were not really prepared for the power that they eventually controlled beyond 1994. With democracy and majority rule now in place, the ANC government over the years seem to wonder what to do with it.

Native South Africans since democracy in 1994 have continued to face a rebranded racial marginalization, oppression, inequality, poverty and repression. To many, it would appear that apartheid only changed skin, because the oppressed people of South Africa are still landless and deprived of the most important factor of production available to them. The land question in South Africa has ridiculed the aspiration of the liberation struggle and tend to reduce the ability and intension of the majority to transition into wealth creation and dignity of their person.

In today's South Africa, the majority and especially young citizens of South Africa have witnessed a gradual but continued desecration of their self-worth through hardship, misery and exploitation of their commonwealth by a few. Native South Africans are as angry today with their political, social and economic conditions as they were during the apartheid regime. Not much has changed. Consequent to that is the transfer of aggression to everyone, anyone that they seek to blame for the misery that has befallen them. The government could not transform the lives of the people positively and the contradictions of splendor, privilege and modernity of a few is still visible against the poverty, pains, landlessness, violence and crime infested community of the majority.

PART 5: AFRICA, KNOW THYSELF

A newspaper headline speaking to Nigeria's contribution to the liberation struggle in South Africa.

Reverse Ubuntu

'They made us leave history, our history, to follow them, right at the back, to follow the progress of their history'

Amilcar Cabral

Ubuntu has long been the philosophy and principle on which the African civilization is justified. Ubuntu is a term commonly used in Southern Africa and particularly in Mzansi to connote and describe our collective humanity. It has been derived from the Bantu dialectics that presents the linkage between human being and the whole of nature, creation, regardless of circumstances. It is a concept of humanity that relates to everything that shows how interconnected human beings are to the material and immaterial.

In several South African languages especially the *Nguni* clan, Ubuntu is translated as 'I am because you are', to suggest that whatever affects you, affects me. It presupposes how we all connect to each other, the environment and nature. Ubuntu is also enshrined in several other ethnicity and languages across Africa and often mean the same thing, but may be called with a different name. Be it *'Mutum'* in Hausa, *Udungu* in Kiswahili, *Ebi* in Yoruba, it reveals and connote to our humanness and interconnectedness. As a statement of fact, very much across Africa the concept of Ubuntu means the same thing, resonates with every African, and it is used to explain every facet of relationship across politics, economy, philosophy, family and the transcendent.

Until recently the idea, principles and philosophy of Ubuntu sits above every tribe, tongue, tradition and behavior of the people of Africa. That is where you find the expression of goodness, harmony, compassion, empathy and reciprocity in every person. It is the foundation standard of the black race that transcends any ideology and belief. It is the way of life inherent in African socialization process and wisdom. Ubuntu is one of the most revered term that determines theory and practice of African oriental civilization for so long that it can be regarded as Africa's keep. There is no such place that Ubuntu exhibited the substance of the struggle for the unity, humanity and opportunities for all Africans by Africans so expressly like in South Africa during the liberation movement. Yet the philosophy and concept of Ubuntu seem to disappear in the deeds and voices of post-apartheid South Africa. Just as it has faded from the attitude and behavior of several Africans across the continent.

It was entirely based on the concept and principle of Ubuntu however, that the Nigerian foreign policy was enacted and on which it re-energized the liberation struggles in Southern Africa. Nigeria got its inspiration to contribute and support the liberation movement on the philosophy of Ubuntu and the mantra that so long as any part of Africa is under colonialism, then every African is under bondage. No African country or its people are free, until every person or country in the continent is free from the shackles of colonialism in any guise. In Ubuntu, everything that affects one affects all, so the principle of Ubuntu guided most of the contributions and commitment that Nigeria put forward over many decades in support of the people of Mzansi to reclaim back their dignity, restore their progress, and sustain their self-worth.

Ubuntu is ideal to venture Africans anywhere in the world of our common good, solidarity of a shared future, and the responsibility that we all hold to protect the black race. It is the guarantee for the pursuit of happiness without hindrance, the right to live anywhere in peace, unity and prosperity with other humans. The philosophy of Ubuntu is a concept of universal benefit to all that are alive to access it, to enjoy it and share in it, as much as it also acknowledges the relevance of the ancestors for creating the circumstance of its existence. There is no way that any African can feel stifled within the continent if the concept and principle of Ubuntu is embedded in our socialization process across African political, social, economic and spiritual structure.

South Africa is the arrow head and precursor of Ubuntu, yet the contradiction and disconnection to ascertain that the concept of Ubuntu is worth presenting on a global scale as the arbiter of African civilization, was starkly a South African anomaly. The tensions and crisis that Africa is undergoing within, and no less the immigrant challenges in South Africa provides a strong argument against Ubuntu, and to even consider if the concept had always been original or domiciled in African civilization. The current human misery and condition in the region and particularly in Nigeria and South Africa have discredited Ubuntu in every facet of human endeavor, whether it be in governance, lifestyle or philosophical growth.

In South Africa specifically, the reasoning behind Ubuntu is absent in the African persona and has not echo on how African leaders and citizens should align, how the responsibility of businesses and clientele should behave, and how statecraft and people across the continent should integrate. The values, virtues and knowledge of

Africa's unique position in the circle of life has become a justification for mobocracy and a perpetual misnomer to its people, their aspiration and prospect. The African people had refused to accept the Ubuntu philosophy or cared to build that which was inherently theirs as a compass to establish the circumstances for personal, communal, countrywide and continental development; ignoring the principle of Ubuntu and not applying it in the presence of African reality had become one of Africa's major developmental indiscretion.

There are calls from many enclaves for a rethink in the application of Ubuntu in public lives of Africans. African communities are increasingly becoming individualist which is a stark contradiction to Ubuntu. It has created a condition of self-fallacy among Africans who are now paying the price of seeing a different image in the mirror and in a constant flux of confusion of who they are, and where to get the self-worth and identity of their being which transcends religion, governance and education. The people of Africa are entirely and constantly viewing 'us' versus 'them', even among indigenes of the same country, let alone citizens of one country in another. These set of people forget that the African sun shines on everything that it touches. Africa is just a bowl of contradiction, unhealthy competition and negative heterogeneity, as a direct consequence of ignoring the ethics of Ubuntu. Ubuntu is very necessary to Africa's development as wood is to a carpenter.

In Ubuntu, African governments are not restricted to providing administration and steering the ship of statecraft alone, but also saddled with providing impetus for good governance. Governments are run by people and these set of people must ensure a very sound understanding of self, community values and a moral standard that could resonate with that of the younger population of citizens, imbibe a culture of family, expression of gratitude, *good* neighborliness, accommodation and peaceful coexistence. Many governments succeed in instilling discipline and collective purpose for development through programs that teach children of their common heritage of how and what the future holds.

The principle of Ubuntu is fading away into oblivion in intra-African interactions because the concept has not been allowed to tinker with the awareness, behavior, attitude and morality of Africans. Ubuntu is seen as an ancient concept or principle that cannot change or transform the continent of Africa into a responsive socialist democracy with modern facilities for a sustained and inclusive opportunities to build a robust livelihood for contemporary life. That is not true. Ubuntu can be used to modernize the thought process of a new era where Africans and especially the young population will seize the ideals of our common and shared humanity to enhance our families, communities and region into a flourishing and powerful domain.

Unfortunately, the political, religious and economic class in Africa have underinvested in the path that puts the people at the center of philosophical and material advantage. This has rubbished any positive outcome that could come from a philosophical rebirth of Ubuntu in molding consciousness of the self upon which the African can compete and display the profound greatness in him or her. Africa became limited by its disadvantages which are innate than exposed, and through an unhurried conspiracy of instilling self-hate and timidity in Africans by interests that knew how much *'amandla'*

Africans could wield should they be allowed to realize the transforming power of their culture and tradition in modern evolution.

The ANC government for whatever reason, do not put priority in articulating people and countries of Africa that hoisted the banner of freedom with them in assistance to defeat apartheid. Even for the value of public interest, the knowledge of people and countries that gave so much for native South Africans to gain political freedom from apartheid is too few on public knowledge, if not skewed. This may have prompted the David Letsoalo (2022) to assert that, 'it was a deliberate effort and ploy to shift the psyche of the excited post-1994 society, poetically branded the 'rainbow nation' from the correct narrative of the revolution of the oppressed people of Azania against colonialism, white supremacy, exploitation and oppression, generally". For the people to know is for them to be aware, and to be aware is for them to understand, to understand eventually breeds tolerance, especially in a vibrant diversity and economic powerhouse that the country has come to mean for every African. Building a rich curriculum on history education is ripe for a time as this.

It may not be a wrong assumption to think that ignorance about African history by Africans themselves is indirectly the reason for many conflicts afflicting the region. No civilization of note could shape its future without respect for historical relationships built by the people. Apart from colonization that has fragmented and disturbed pre-existing relationships in Africa, contemporary efforts to build back the continent and unite its people did not succeed in detaching itself from the sentiments and opinion of non-Africans and the systems they left behind.

The African Renaissance

At the dawn of the 21st century, African leaders started believing in their ability to transform the continent through a sound knowledge and identity, philosophical direction and the apparent need to integrate its people and establish the continent on a path to sustainable development. This was the era when a crop of African politicians and thinkers like Olusegun Obasanjo, Thabo Mbeki, Abdulahi Wade, Meles Zanawi, Muammar Gaddafi and others were running the affairs of Africa. In fact, it was Obasanjo and Mbeki as mentioned, that came close to bringing Africans together through a political fiat in establishing the New Partnership for African Development (NEPAD), Nigeria South Africa Biennial Commission, and to reinvigorate the regional body of the African Union. This period witnessed a rising Africa acknowledged even beyond the shores of the continent. It was the decade of the African renaissance.

When former president Thabo Mbeki of South Africa commenced the 'African Renaissance, as a call for an African rebirth and renewal, it stimulated academic and philosophical rationale on how to situate the theory and practice of such concept. In this period Africa was beginning to understand its place, to carve a niche for itself in the global community and call for a rebirth of the African wholesomeness which was needed to build an indigenous system that is run by Africans for Africa. It resonated with the people of Africa because African renaissance was actually a *de ja vu*, something they seem to already know, or understand when the same call for the unity and progress of Africa was sang by strong personalities like Kwame Nkrumah, Nnamdi Azikiwe, Amical Cabral, etc.

African renaissance had become the umbrella word of an Africanist agenda in the twenty first century that will usher an era of African development experienced through positive progress, cohesion and a people driven interaction across every sector and along a vertical and horizontal systems that is created, determined and influenced by African themselves.

This is not the first time that Africans heard voices calling for an African renaissance. The unity and integration of the black race had been submitted many years ago by Cheikh Anta Diop of Senegal, Kwame Nkrumah of Ghana, and even Marcus Garvey of the USA and great singers like Bob Nesta Marley and Fela Anikulapo-Kuti. These great African scholars had written and called for the unity and development of Africa through the logic of the African renaissance. Even though in scholarly terms, the call for an African Renaissance was argued to be a duplicate of what has happened in other climes especially in Europe, and that it was nothing original to Africa. This gave many people to snub the idea and its conceptualization to implementation. But when Thabo Mbeki reintroduced the African renaissance during his tenure as South African president, he became one among many political leaders in Africa that spoke eloquently of the progress in people of Africa through the benefits of unity, integration, identity and the pride in the black race.

Again, borrowed from Cheikh Anta Diop, Thabo Mbeki echoed in the African renaissance a principle of accommodation. Africa should be home to any person of black origin and everyone who live within it. There is no sense for any African to feel insecure or unloved inside the continent, as it is important for the black race anywhere in the world to consider Africa as a place of rest and security. The concept of the African renaissance should be broken down to several aspects that would encourage acceptance of our collective origin, dignity, identity, color and humanity. The African renaissance does not only show how to reconstruct the African identity in front of the international community, but it is also to teach Africans how to speak, listen, behave and accommodate each other. It must provide the connection across African languages, cultures, education, cooperation and distinctiveness.

Africa has relied over centuries on oral transfer of knowledge. This was also the strategy that has been one of the basic means of informal education available to young Africans during the liberation struggle. The elders used oral literatures to teach, entertain, inform and enlightened the younger generation of their place in life. The 21st century however reveals a noticeable decline in oral knowledge transfer by family, community, government and everyone saddled with such responsibility, and with it came also a decline in self-worth and awareness. Oral history is relegated to extinction as African stories of no distant past have become bleak and opaque. Interesting books written about different regions of Africa like K.B.C Onwobiko's School Certificate History of West Africa (1977), Dani Nabudere's Afrikology: Philosophy and Wholeness. An Epistemology (2011) and Ali Mazrui's The African (1986) among many others. These books and essays are written and are an interesting read, but many young Africans have lost interest in books and seeking knowledge about their history, conditions and heritage. Majority of youthful population are not aware or even remember where they are coming from, with so much uncertainty of their place in the world. There is no African story that dictate their step into the future.

Every hierarchy of the society should accept the concept of the African renaissance even if it will be done simply by storytelling. The absence of this ingredient of value to the development of Africa must be blamed on African governments for not taking the most of it into account. Senior citizens in Africa go to their graves with abundant and accumulated knowledge of events that had shaped the past and influenced the present, yet did not deem it fit to share this knowledge across to the up-and-coming generation. This has produced gaps in understanding and appreciation of memory, self-knowledge and identity in the development planning of African societies. No doubt, story-telling of African philosophy and culture was a strong attribute of African forbearers and its usage and impact has been felt more in the African-American societies in the USA than in Africa itself. The value of transferring history to individual, national and regional consciousness is one sure way to build the African renaissance.

African renaissance is also to further encourage a positive outlook and share in commonness, even though conscious of our uniqueness. The history of Africa has witnessed a balkanization of the vision, identity, civilization and values in the people, but there is still a great deal of the core of African-ness in the attitude, disposition and character of the black race, anywhere, anytime and any anyhow. Whether it is from a traditional or modern logic, African renaissance should be the yardstick of measuring Africanism in every sphere of endeavor especially on black-on-black affiliations. It is of concern when some Africans do not fully understand African renaissance to mean a collective responsibility. Some native South Africans do see African renaissance as a wish list or a process to entrench black leadership over white dominance in every sector of Mzansi. African renaissance is beyond that, it is bigger than just the quest for dominance. It is the framework and base of the consciousness in every African. It is Africa's blue print towards self-actualization, collective purpose and sustainable development.

That is why the political, cultural, scientific and technical advancement of Africa will depend on the entrenchment of a deep sense of philosophical identity that will propel interaction with the personhood of who is an African and why the African renaissance is necessary for reinvigorating the position of the black race in the quality of humanity. Embedded in the African renaissance is the concept of Ubuntu which has to interact with other factors to build the fortunes of African commonwealth, growth, advancement and development.

It would seem that some citizens of Mzansi do not understand that African Renaissance is a statement of negritude, of empathy, accommodation, solidarity, forgiveness, community advancement and all that makes the black person significant. The tragedy of this realization is that many people view themselves from the spectacle of colonialism which has further sectionalized the continent and its people. African renaissance is the essence of Africanism, of the social order of things and how every black person should relate with the each other. Hence if Ubuntu is an African indigenous system, then the African renaissance is the framework on which it can be used to advocate and project for an African way of life in the global community.

Whether it be a term to restore the agenda for a political, economic and socio-cultural unity of Africans or not, the African renaissance must hold a universal meaning to any black man, woman and child.

In its application, it should be the yardstick for African cooperation, emancipation and authentication of the Negro identity. There is no place therefore that such inclusive identity should abide than with the beautiful people of South Africa. The people of Mzansi must see other Africans as a reflection of themselves and also accept the aspirations of Africans as the ultimate reason for the African renaissance.

The deep meaning of the African renaissance can only make sense in practice, when every citizen of Africa is allowed residence in any location within the continent regardless of colonial demarcation inherent in countries and statehood. The black person should be able to live in any community, anywhere in Africa without fear, intimidation and prejudice. The impression of some South Africans that the more southern other Africans come in search of better livelihood or habitation, translates to job loses, fewer women to date and the spread of diseases and reduced opportunities for the natives is not correct. Taking up residence in any part of Africa could be of immense advantage to the host community if such is understood in the spirit of African renaissance.

Africanist perspective to development often stand in contradiction to most western prescription of global development. However, pursuing development with Ubuntu at its core makes it easier to understand the moral and philosophical foundation behind the Africanist mandate. During apartheid in Southern Africa generally, Nigeria was able to use capitalism as a weapon to extinguish the substance of oppression inherent in the western idea of subjugation for individual gains. The reality and aspiration of Africanism could not allow Nigeria turn a blind eye on the suffering of other Africans during apartheid. This has become a classic example of how the African renaissance manifest.

In the spirit of Africanism, Nigeria recognized the significance of what NEPAD stood for and the African renaissance project became the rallying point in facilitating a motion of forward looking and progressive people towards prosperity. It was during the African renaissance that the continent was termed 'African rising' by many western clouts as Africa and its people displayed a fervent potential for growth. Many African countries were described as emerging economies with enormous promise to improve the quality of life of its people. The system currently in use has not shown proper direction for African renaissance within the continent, even when political leadership of the day keep coming with similar strategy that will unite Africa and plant it deeply into the soil of inclusive and sustainable growth and development.

Nigeria-South Africa Day

There were significant events that happened during the liberation struggle to which Nigeria and South Africa can remember and celebrate with pride. It can be a single event or a collection thereof that both countries could deliberately adopt and set aside to be acknowledged about the liberation struggle that holds a historical value to both countries. Several examples can be used to immortalize the liberation struggle from the point of view of the friendship between Nigeria and South Africa. For instance, the day that the Nigerian government established the Southern Africa Relief Fund (SARF) could be used as a day of significance to reiterate Nigeria South African friendship, or be declared a Nigeria-South Africa diurnal.

The SARF was a contribution that the Nigerian government made to the people of South Africa as a medium to promote, build and prepare the citizens of South Africa with the capacity to take back their country from the white minority government in Pretoria. It was conceived as a charitable gesture towards ameliorating the sufferings of South Africans, but later became a symbolic tool in asserting the culture of resistance against oppression. The SARF offered financial support to rebuild places and memories of value that have been destroyed by the apartheid government in South Africa. It also offered scholarship and training for young ANC members to study in Nigerian universities, receive quality education and return back to Mzansi, armed with capacity to replace the oppressive regime that has kept the native majority in perpetual ignorance, lack and despondency. The SARF was instrumental to several successes that was recorded in the entire history of the liberation struggle even within South Africa at the time, and across other regions in Africa that have ANC regional offices.

Thanks to historical and documented facts, several events that occurred in the course of the liberation struggle could have been lost for the young generation. Some actors of the liberation struggle have died and may not have told their experiences of the anti-apartheid movement to young South Africans. Thankfully, some citizens of Mzansi are still alive to encourage using historical events as value to bolster Nigeria and South African relations. In the words of Lungi Daweti, a beneficiary of the SARF who acquired university education in Nigeria during the apartheid era and have made friends with some notable Nigerians as students, said that "both John and I belonged to what was known as the Nigeria-ANC Friendship and Cultural Association. The association comprised civil society membership ranging from tertiary students, lecturers, Nigerian workers belonging to unions affiliated to the Nigerian Labor Congress, church organizations, artistes, business people, lawyers, etc…(sic) those were the times when the chief representative of the ANC in West Africa was the late comrade Zinjiva Nkondo who was then known as Victor Matlou and married to Sankie Mthembi-Mahanyele, then known as Rebecca Matlou, who was the administrative secretary in the ANC office. She later became the second national minister of Housing in a democratic South Africa". (Benson Upah and Onah Iduh: 2010).

These historical truth of impactful friendship may not be worth noting if Nigeria and South Africa do not make any attempt to build a better future from its past. The past should be understood to guide the journey to the future of Africans into building a formidable and progressive knowledge base system for generations to come. The history doesn't have to exclude the unfortunate stories of oppression, lack, under-development and misgivings of the past, but to also acknowledge the friendship, support, resilience and resistance to foreign induced misery of which every African country and people have its fair share, and of which Africa overcame through unity of purpose and brotherhood.

There is nothing wrong if the Nigeria-South Africa Biennial Commission set up by Obasanjo and Thabo Mbeki deem it fit to set a day apart from the facts of the liberation struggle as a remembrance of friendship, brotherhood and the contributions that either of the country have done to its people in particular, and the citizens of Africa in general. This can inculcate in Africans the spirit of love for one another, a sense of collective empathy and responsibility, and a knowledge driven society. History is always important to the future of any person, society or country. The government and people of both Nigeria and South Africa must find it imperative to keep the history of the liberation struggle as a positive reminder of our collective destiny. Let there be a day of Africa, when all people and countries will celebrate friendship with a fellow African country, based on history of a good deed or friendship cultivated. It will surprise us to know what history will reveal about the good relationship initiated by African forebears.

The governments of Nigeria and South Africa need to appreciate how far we have come in building a sense of belonging for the black race. There were so many aspects of collaboration that South Africa and Nigeria have shown great promise. The greatness of Africa will be revealed and boosted by saying or doing little things that may not seem to matter in statecraft, but very significant in opening windows of association, appreciation and revive the hope for continued friendship and mutual respect. Expressing gratitude between sovereign countries is an ingredient in constructivism and it unlocks the opportunities that supports and build friendship, acceptable conducts in human interactions and international relations.

Some may say that everything about apartheid is now in the past and we should put it behind us. True as that might be, the fact that little or no mention of the great valor that Nigeria displayed during the period of apartheid in South Africa over the years has created bad blood and distorted what could have been a deliberate effort at promoting peace and a people centered African interaction between two very important countries in Africa. It is very sad that an option to stay quiet when words should be spoken about past rapport has made an 'enemy' of African brotherhood and ridiculed a deliberate investment of Africa relations.

It is also due to widespread ignorance and hidden truths about the camaraderie established during the liberation struggles that no Nigerian name has adorned any street in South Africa like it was given to other freedom fighters and political leaders of some African countries. Not that it matters, but acknowledging history could show how Africans appreciate themselves, why they need to tolerate one another and enhance bond towards a renaissance. In a way, gratitude could unlock the fullness of the African spirit to deliver more blessings to the way of life of the African, just as it will make Africans appreciate how far we have come and clarity and on the journey ahead of all.

The quality of the African mindset needs to be drawn from a sincere appreciation of history and a conscious pool of goodwill that we all must generate to feed our future. For a very long time, Africans see themselves from stories told by foreign elements which in most cases are untrue, undetailed or meant to stoke unhealthy interactions. This situation has dampened any effort at reviving the hope and sense of belonging that Africans are known for. There could never be a condition of mutual respect, communication and common destiny if Africans do not see the need to be pure in their impression of one another, and this could come from the appreciation of tangible and intangible interactions.

Genuinely showing gratitude to Nigeria for their role in ending apartheid is not in any way to make Mzansi feel indebted to Nigeria. In a broader sense, saying or showing gratitude will only make Nigeria and South Africa relations authentic and not the seeming downcast interface between the people of these countries. The connection between the people of Nigeria and South Africa does not produce a feeling of profound friendship but of an under-valued sense of recognition. Self-recognition could simply create a feeling of supra-national awareness and worth and improve mutual tendency to grow together, protect each other's interest, build and increase the confidence in each other. By implication, it will certainly re-align our interest in domestic and international issues, substitute doubt and envy for goodwill and collective bargaining.

Native South Africans are welcoming and love to enjoy the good things of life, just like any other nationality on the continent. Their current attitude to others is however interfering with the values and identity to share in the benefits of life. This is further worsened by a government who deem it unnecessary to set out on a deliberate ambition to heal its people from the hurt and embarrassment of apartheid through the dissemination of knowledge of whom and how the success of overcoming its darkest moments may be measured. Being the only country under a white minority rule way into the twentieth century, South Africans have not been told of its struggles from the lens of other Africans, who incidentally stood by them through thick and thin to end apartheid.

The acknowledgment that many Nigerians demand from the highest to the lowest stratum of the South African society about their contributions in ending apartheid will not be about indebtedness or patting the back of Nigeria or boosting its ego, but it is about setting a good history of African solidarity and encouraging better cooperation and mutual understanding among Africans. Understanding does not come in a vacuum but could be cultivated using frequent and deliberate discussion about friendship that has been allowed to thrive without holding anything back.

Acknowledging or sometimes constantly reiterating a historical good, even as done in the past could be a very viable strategy for potential friendship and cooperation between an individual, group or countries and could form the basis for cohesion for an expanded international cooperation and development. Recognizing a good deed is part of a principle of Ubuntu and is shrouded in every oriental culture and has been a tool to promote friendship, accommodation, integrity and progress among people. That may explain why for instance, the Chinese government always remind the African people at every opportunity of the friendship that both people have cultivated in the past and how this friendship holds the potential for a better future together. According to a Chinese proverbs, 'to attract good fortune, spend a new coin on an old friend, share an old pleasure with a new friend, and lift up the heart of a true friend by writing his name on the wings of the dragon'.

To constantly remind ourselves of what made us a human family is to imprint in our consciousness the need to create the space for each other to coexist by showing appreciation where it is necessary. Nigeria and South Africa are very important countries who have the fate of the black race in their stride. There will be no sacrifice too big for both countries to dispense in order to restore and promote the dignity of other Africans and show genuine love for each other.

Let Nigeria and South Africa amplify what makes us human or more specifically what makes us Africans. There are sets of codes that shape our behaviour and construct our social ideals. In Ubuntu, part of its principle is the ability to appreciate goodness and even admit to how such good deed has endeared loyalty and potential for future alliance. An example of such could be an act of kindness or a word of thanks to appreciate a good deed. It seems little, but appreciation goes a long way in demonstrating togetherness and every advantage that comes with it.

The magnanimity of Nigeria towards a sister country of South Africa appears to be forgotten by the beneficiaries. The benevolence is hardly acknowledged not to speak of expecting a vote of gratitude from the government and people of Mzansi. There is a great deal of political, economic and social capital that is derived from acknowledging a good deed by a friendly country to another. Whether such deed was done in the past or in the present, the receiving country benefits as much as the country extending such good deed. There are several reasons why some countries and its people could feel less threatened by each other regardless of whether they share divergent views on any aspect of domestic and international issues.

Incidentally, the policy of silence about Nigeria's contribution towards ending apartheid in South Africa is a missed opportunity in repairing the love hate relationship that has troll the people of Nigeria and South Africa. The government of both countries should invest in platforms to immortalize, identify and appreciate the firm relationship of the past in order to express confidence in current and future alliance. Nigeria and South Africa need each other in a way that could only be determined by its people, and acknowledging historical friendship with honesty, mutual respect and sacrifice for each other will create a solidarity to live for and which will benefit everyone.

It is important for the people and government of Mzansi to create the thoroughfare in embracing other Africans by making deliberate statements in words, deeds or murals to enlighten their younger generation of an important part of their history-the history of their struggle and the path that led to victory - victory won by the support that South Africa got from the friends of freedom. Africa should draw strength from the past and forge a quality future for its citizens, out of a genuine determination to meet the current and future aspiration of the people.

Government to government collaboration must be deconstructed to promote more interface among the people of both countries in a more lucrative manner. Is it any wonder that at the entertainment industry, the cooperation of the people of South Africa and Nigeria has always been highly rated. Is it in music, cultures or drama, the alliance between these two countries have produced the best content and raised the standard in Africa. There is no doubt that lack of any deliberate and conscious effort by the government of South Africa to recognize the notable contributions of Nigeria and other notable countries in the continent have created a gulf of misunderstanding, misgiving, and diversity in shambles for Africa.

Bibliography

Olayiwola Abegunrin (2009). *Nigeria and the Struggle for the Liberation of South Africa, In; Africa in Global Politics in the Twenty-First Century.* Palgrave, Macmillan, New York.

Emeka Aniagolu (2021). *Rainbow Nation: A Historical and Sociopolitical Analysis of Apartheid, Anti-Apartheid Struggle, Post-Apartheid Conditions and Contemporary Xenophobia in Republic of South Africa.* Fahimta Books

Ibrahim Babangida (1991). *For Their Tomorrow, We Gave Our Today: Selected Speeches of IBB.* Volume II. Spectrum Books

Lawrence A. Blum & Victor J. Seidler (1989). *A Truer Liberty: Simone Weil and Marxism.* Critical Social Thought. Routledge, New York

Nancy L. Clark and William H. Worger (2022). *South Africa: The Rise and Fall of Apartheid.* (4th Edition). London

Steve Clark (ed) (1993). *Nelson Mandela Speaks. Forging a democratic non-racial South Africa.* Pathfinder Press

Fathima Nduka Eze (2012). *Joe Garba's Legacy (Eds): Thirty-Two selected Speeches and Lectures on National Governance, Confronting Apartheid and Foreign Policy.* Xlibris Corporation

Joseph Garba (1987). *Diplomatic Soldiering: Nigeria Foreign Policy, 1975-1979.* Spectrum

Joseph Hanlon (1986). *Apartheid's Second Front: South Africa's War Against its Neighbours.* Penguin Books. New Zealand

Attahiru Jega and Jacqueline Farris (2010). *Nigeria at Fifty: Contributions to Peace, Democracy and Development.* Yar'Adua Foundation.

Lebo Keswa (2015). *Lest We Forget...Africa's Hospitality Liberated South Africa*. The Guardian; City File: 26 April 2015.guardian.ng

W.A de Klerk (1975). *The Puritans in Africa*. R. Collings. London W1

David Letsoalo (2022). *In Search of Meaning of the June 1976 Soweto Uprisings in the Context of the Liberation Struggle*. Sunday Independent (Analysis). Iol.co.za/sundayindependent

Dani Nabudere (2011). *Afrikology, Philosophy and Wholeness: An Epistemology*. Africa Institute of South Africa

Nic Rhoodie (1972). *South African Dialogue: Contrast in South African Thinking on Basic Race Issues*. Johannesburg. McGraw

Ebrahim Salie (2012). *Analysis of the Voortrekker Monument. Revised Version*. Cape Town, South Africa. www.academia.edu

Pierre du Toit (1995). *State Building and Democracy in Southern Africa: Botstwana, Zimbabwe and South Africa*. United States Institute for Peace. USIP Press. Washington DC, USA.

JK Shinkaiye (2002). *The African Union and the Challenges of Cooperation and Integration: Proceedings of the National Seminar*; Ministry of Integration and Cooperation in Africa. Abuja. May 14 & 15 2002.

Stockholm International Peace Research Institute (1976). *Southern Africa: The Escalation of a Conflict. A Politico-Military Study*. (SIPRI)

Desmond Tutu (1994). *The Rainbow People of God: South Africa's Victory Over Apartheid*. Edited by John Allen. Transworld Publishers. London.

Benson Upah and Onah Iduh (2010). *Homage to Commitment: Tribute to John Odah at 50*. Panaf Press

Index

A

Abacha, General Sani of Nigeria, 5
General Abacha sent $10 million to Mandela to cover expenses of the inauguration ceremony, 111, 135

Abdul-Jabbar, Omale Allen, a Cerebral Personality, my friend and brother, the award-winning writer and functionary of the Association of Nigerian Authors (ANA), viii

Abegunrin, Olayiwola (2009), 12, 42, 59

Achebe, Prof. Chinua, 124

Action Against Apartheid World Conference, 103

Adichie, Chimamanda Ngozi, I believe in storytelling, 35

Africa Has Come of Age: Speech by Murtala Muhammed at the OAU January, 11, 1976, 78-80

Africa, Know Thyself, 143

Africa: Call to action, 59

African National Congress, ix, 14, 21, 69
Pixley Ka Isaka Seme (Founder of the African National Congress), 14
Biggest beneficiary of the liberation struggle and have been in power since 1994, 22
How ANC muted the contributions of Nigeria to the liberation struggle, 23
Native South Africa Native National Congress now African National Congress, 52
Umkhonto we sizwe (MK) the youth wing of ANC, 53
Actors like ANC, 69
ANC political School, 135

African Renaissance, 30-31, 140, 151-157

African Rising, 157

African Union (AU) formerly Organization of African Unity (OAU), 64, 78,

Afrikaner Nationalism and the Class/Racial/Ethnic character of the anti-apartheid movement, 27

Afrocentric version of the liberation struggle is vital, 58

Agyeno, Dr. Oboshi, x-xi
Interviewed the people of South Africa from Pretoria to Limpopo, the Free State to Kwazulu Natal, 11

Africa must tell its story, 30

Akinyemi, Prof. Bolaji, 94

Amandla Africans, 149

Amaechi, Chief Madubike
Accommodated Nelson Mandela for six months in Lagos, Nigeria at the request of Dr. Nnamdi Azikiwe, 61

Angelou, Maya, 3

Anglo-Boer war in 1900, 35, 37

Angola,
Contributors to the liberation struggle in South Africa, 21

Aniagolu, Emeka: 2021, 43, 46, 60

Anikulapo-Kuti, Fela, 124, 152

Anyaoku, Chief Emeka
Former Secretary General of the Commonwealth of Nations, 7-8

Apartheid regime in South Africa, ix, 11
Final liquidation of apartheid, x

Post-apartheid history of South Africa, x

Inappropriate documentation of Nigeria's role in the liberation struggle, xi

Dismantling of apartheid in South Africa, xi, 99, 118

Collapse of apartheid and resultant Xenophobia, xi

South African youths unaware of the Pan African spirit that pioneered the liberation struggle, xi

The role of Nigerian diplomacy in the liberation struggle, xii

Many native South Africans aren't aware of the contributions of Nigeria or other friends of freedom against apartheid South Africa, 12

Exploit of African Countries in the apartheid movement, 12, 15

Impact of the policy of segregation in South Africa, 16

South African media dominated by white supremacist and their cohort, 22

Creating an awareness of the history of decolonization of Africa, 30

Arguably the most racist administration in Africa's modern history, 31

The hypocrisy of the United States and the United Kingdom, 43

Apartheid became a war declared by the white minority against the majority, 48

Liberation struggle was fought on two main fronts, 54

Nigeria regarded apartheid as a crime against humanity, 70

Index

The struggle is being planned and executed by terrorist cum communist organizations, 79

Attahiru Jega (2010), 57

Awolowo, Chief Obafemi, 77

Azania, 13, 44, 150

Azikiwe, Dr. Nnamdi, then Governor General of Nigeria, 61, 77, 151

B

Babangida, Ibrahim (1991:252), 65

Balewa, Alhaji Tafawa, ix, 25, 77

Bantustan, 15-16
  Bantu and Khoi-San women, 36, 45
  Bantustan Policy, 46

Bello, Ahmadu, 77

Benson Upah and Onah Idu: 2010, 159

Bibliography, 167-168

Biko, Stephen Bantu, 13, 14, 55, 77

Blum, Lawrence and Victor Seidler (1989), 31

Bob Nesta Marley, 152

Boers, 36-40; 46-47; 139
  They made sure they have legal backing to give legitimacy for their action and coercion, 46

"Born Free" South Africa Youths, 6, 8

Botha, Peter, 86

Botswana, 5, 68, 78, 88

Brazil
  Supported the liberation struggle in South Africa, 67

British Petroleum
  Assets nationalized by Nigeria (31 July, 1979), 87

Buthelezi, Mangosuthu of Inkatha Freedom party, 8

C

Cabral, Amical, 77, 145, 151

Cape Colony and Natal
  Two British colonies that joined to create the modern South African State, 35

Cape of Good Hope, 36-37

Cartwright, Justin (1977), 39

China, People Republic of (PRC), 47, 67

Clark, Akporode, 97

Clark, Nancy and William Worger (2022), 46

Cole, Dr. Dele, vii

Commonwealth
  The expulsion of apartheid South Africa from the commonwealth in 1961, xi

Commonwealth Eminent Persons Group, 76, 116

Commonwealth Games, 102

Congress of South African Trade Unions (COSATU), 62, 84

D

David Letsoalo (2022), 22, 40, 150

Daweti, Lungi, 159

Dedication, v

De Klerk, W. A (1975), 35, 37

Diop, Cheikh Anta, 115, 152

Diplomacy: multilateral and Backchannel, 95
Africanization agenda in Nigeria's diplomacy, 98

Dlamini,
Nobody helped us during apartheid, 3

Activist and local Champion of Post-apartheid South Africa, 5

Documentary Evidence,
Few are available in South Africa to tell versions of Nigeria's contributions to the liberation struggles, 66

Dube, John, 52-53

Dutch East India Company, 44

E

Ebrahim Salie: 2012, 38

Egypt,
Contributors to the Liberation struggle in South Africa, 21

Ejinaka, Amb. John, vii, xii

Enahoro, Anthony, 77

Emeka Aniagolu: 2021, 7-8, 43, 46, 60, 76

Eswatini (Swaziland), 88

Ethiopia,
Contributors of the liberation struggle in South Africa, 21

F

Fela Anikulapo-Kuti, 124, 152

Fellowship of Brotherhood, 107

Festival of Black Arts and Culture (FESTAC)
Hosted by Nigeria in 1977 was a platform Nigeria exploited to rally African artist and culture ambassadors against apartheid, 70

Ford, President General of USA, 78

France, 49, 72-73

Freedom Park and Union Building, 124, 140

Frontline State (FLS), x-xi,
Nigeria was considered a frontline State even though not geographically located in Southern Africa, 68, 92

G

Gaddafi, Muamma of Libya, 5, 7, 136, 151

Gambari, Prof. Ibrahim, vii, 97, 100

Garba, Joe (2012), 27-29, 39, 39, 77, 97
Chair of the UN Special committee against apartheid and President of UNGA, 95, 115

Garvey, Marcus, 152

Ghana,
Contributors to the liberation struggle in South Africa, 21

Gowon, Gen. Yakubu, 77

Great Trek (Vortrekker), 37-38, 49

Green land and Distant Rainbow, 113

Group Area Act, 46

Guinea, 109-110

Guinea Bissau, 77

H

Hani, Chris, 14

Hanlon, Joseph, 87-88, 90

Harriman, Leslie O, 97

I

Ikoku, S.G
Chairman, Nigerian National Action Committee Against Apartheid, 63

India,
Supported the Liberation struggle in South Africa, 67

Indirect Rule and Assimilation Systems adopted by the British and French in Africa, 48-49

Inkatha Freedom Party of Mangosuthu Buthlezi, 8

Institute for Dispute Resolution in Africa (IDRA) now the Thabo Mbeki School of public and International Affairs University of South Africa, vii

International Labour Organization (ILO)
Nigeria became a member in 1961, 21

Nigeria moved the proposal that expelled apartheid South Africa from ILO, 1964, 21

J

Jan Van Riebeeck
The European character that they claim founded South African, 36

Jega, Attahiru (2010), 57

Joe Garba (2012), 27-29, 39, 39, 77, 97

John Dube, 52-53

Jonas, Chief Iche Udeji, 135

Joseph Hanlon (1986), 87-88, 90

Justin Cartwright (1977), 39

K

Kangaroo Court
  Mandela arrested and tried through Kangaroo Court and sentenced to life imprisonment, 62

Kaunda, Kenneth of Zambia, 4, 77, 136

Keswa, Lebo: 2015, 42

Khadiagala, Gilbert, 92

Khama, Seretse of Botswana, 5, 78

Khoi San and Bantu Africans, 36, 45

King Moshoeshoe, 52

King Shaka, 52

Kissinger, Henry
  American Secretary of State, 80-82

Klerk, W. A de (1975), 35, 37

L

Land Amendment Act, 46

Last Authority
  Captured as the title of this book is figurative and deliberate, 12

  This is a historical narrative of the liberation struggle in South Africa from the paint, brush and canvas of Nigeria, 13

Lebo Keswa: 2015, 42

Lesotho, 88

Letsoalo, David: 2022, 22, 40, 150

Libya,
  Contributors to the liberation struggle in South Africa, 21

Lithuli, Albert, 14, 53

Louis Trichardt "Great Trek", 38

Lungi Daweti, 159

M

Macaulay, Herbert, 77

Machel, Samora of Mozambique, 4, 78, 90, 136

Mahlangu, Solomon, 14, 55

Makeba, Miriam 1961, 3, 55-56, 73
  Sang in honour of Murtala Muhammed, 140

Malawi, 87

Mama Africa: *See Miriam Makeba*; 82

Mandela, President Nelson, 9, 14, 18, 20, 53, 55, 61
  Mandela stayed for six months at No. 5 Okotie Eboh Street Ikoyi, Lagos State, accommodated by Chief Madubike Amaechi in 1963, 61

  Arrested and tried through a Kangaroo Court and sentenced to life imprisonment, 62

General Sani Abacha sent $10 Million to Nelson Mandela to cover expenses of the inauguration ceremony, 111

Mandela Tax in Nigeria, 120

Marcus Garvey, 152

Marley, Bob Nesta, 152

Mashinini, Tebeho, 14, 34, 56, 83, 90, 109-110
Assassinated in Guinea, 109

Matlou, Mrs. Boshigo,
A South African who lived, schooled and worked in Nigeria during the apartheid era, vii

Rebecca Matlou married to Victor Matlou, 159

Known as Sankie Mthembi–Mahanyele before her marriage to Victor Matlou, 159

Matlou, Rebecca, 159

Matlou Victor, 159
Was later known as Zinjiva Nkondo, 159

Maya Angelou, 3

Mazrui, Ali, 153

Mbeki, Govan, 14

Mbeki, Thabo
Former President of South Africa, 7, 151

Lived in Nigeria for seven years, 109

Miriam Makeba 1961, 3, 55-56, 73
Sang in honor of Murtala Muhammed, 140

Mofokeng, Major General Daniel, Head of the SANDF Foreign Relations, 42

Mohammed, Salisu Nuhu,
Former acting General Secretary, Nigeria Labour Congress, 63

Mozambique, 4, 59, 68, 78, 88-90, 92, 93, 109, 136

Muhammed, Murtala of Nigeria, 4, 78-80, 82, 104, 140
Africa has come of age, 77, 80

Mzansi
A slang word used by natives whose connotation means "South", 13-15, 18, 25, 28, 29, 36, 38, 43, 46, 48, 49, 52, 56, 58, 60, 63, 64, 86, 89, 110, 122, 123, 125, 127, 135, 136, 145, 146, 154-156, 158, 159, 162, 164, 165

N

Nabudare, Dani, 153

Namibia,
Nigeria's role helped in bringing political freedom to Namibia and Angola, 68

Nancy Clark and William Worger (2022), 46

National Association of Nigerian Students (NANS), 63

National Party
  Introduced the apartheid system in 1948, 15-16

Nationalization of multinational corporations belonging to key super powers, xi, 81, 83-84
  Assets of British Petroleum nationalized by Nigeria, 84

  Barclays Bank nationalized 85

Netherlands, The, 16
  The Calvinist Dutch of Netherlands, 35

  Implantation of the Dutch in Africa, 36

  Dutch citizens who later preferred to be called Boers (meaning farmers), 35

  Dutch war of independence against Philip II of Spain (W. A de Klerk 1975: pp. 3-9), 37

  Boers ultimately came to refer themselves as the Afrikaners, 40

  Sailors from Netherlands, 44

  Had to cut ties with their kindred in South Africa, 67

New partnership for Africa Development (NEPAD), 127, 151, 157

Nigeria,
  Three decades of Nigeria's contributions to the liberation struggle in South Africa, iv

Alhaji Tafawa Balewa, Nigerian Prime Minister at the time, in 1961, reacted to the Sharpeville massacre, ix

Various Nigerian Government widened the scope of Participation, x

Every Nigerian both in cash and kind contributed towards the liberation struggle in South Africa, x

South African freedom fighters were provided with Nigerian International passport, x

Nigeria's leading role in the liberation struggle earned her membership of the frontline states, x

Inappropriate documentation of the role of Nigeria in the liberation struggle, xi

Nationalization of British assets by the Nigerian Government, xi, 81, 83-84

South African Youths unaware of Nigeria's leading role in the liberation struggle of South Africa, xii

The role of Nigerian diplomacy at all levels in the collective fight for the liberation of South Africa, xii

Africanist posture of Nigeria foreign policy in the liberation struggle of Southern Africa, 10

Many native South Africans aren't aware of the contribution of Nigeria or other friends of freedom against apartheid South Africa, 12

Nigeria in the 1970s, 1980s, and 1990s was the last period that many remembered in deeds and words of how truly powerful and manifest Nigeria was in Africa, 13

Nigeria's influential role in closing the chapter of apartheid in Africa 18

Information about Nigeria's role should be recognized through story telling, 20

Nigeria contributions to the liberation struggle from the 1970s, 20

Nigeria became a member of the International Labour Organization (ILO) in 1961, 21

How the African National Congress (ANC) muted the contributions of Nigeria to the liberation struggle in South Africa, 23

Nigeria's capitalist-oriented entity was seen by oppressed South Africans who were psyched up by communist system hence the disdain, 25

Nigeria's contributions of political goodwill, material and financial assistance made tremendous impact to the liberation struggle, 26

Call to rise against apartheid became louder in Nigeria by the 1970s, 60

Liberation struggles during the Murtala/Obasanjo regimes, 62

Nigeria Labour Congress, 62-63

Trade Union Congress of Nigeria, 63

Nigeria adopted and Africanization posture in relation to South Africa, 64

Few documentary evidences are available in South Africa to tell versions of Nigeria's contributions to the liberation struggles, 66

Nigeria was considered a Frontline state x

Nigeria regarded apartheid as a crime against humanity, 70

Nigeria's hardline support and killing of Murtala Muhammed, 80

Nationalization of multinational corporation belonging to key super powers, xi, 81, 83-84

Matching words with actions over apartheid, 81

Nigeria became the new global hub of anti-apartheid movement, 83

Nigeria contributed a total of about US$61 Billion to support the end of apartheid, 93

Nigeria headed the UN Special Committee against Apartheid for 30 years, 99

Africa, the center-piece of Nigeria's foreign policy, 107

Gen. Abacha sent $10 million to Nelson Mandela to cover expenses of the inauguration ceremony, 101

Southern African Relief Funds (SAFR), 120

Nigeria's contributions earned her a loathsome persona from the people of South Africa, 125

Policy of silence about Nigeria's contributions towards ending apartheid, 165

Nigeria-ANC Friendship and cultural Association, 159

Nigeria South Africa Biennial Cooperation, 127, 151

Nigeria-South Africa Day, 158

Nigerian Labour Congress, 62-63

Nigerian National Action Committee against Apartheid (NACAP), 63

S. G. Ikoku, Chairman, 63

Nigeria Voice Newspaper: 2013, 110

Nkomati Accord, 90

Nkondo, Zinjiva, 159
   He is also known as Victor Matlou, 159

Nkrumah, Kwame of Ghana, 5, 7, 26, 77, 109, 136, 137, 151, 152

Nollywood (Nigerian Movies), 116

Nyerere, Julius former, President of Tanzania, 4, 5, 7, 25, 26, 77, 136, 137

O

Obasanjo, Gen. Olusegun, 62, 76, 77, 80, 116, 120, 121, 140, 151, 160
   Contributed to the Southern Africa Relief Fund, 120, 158

Oboshi Agyeno, Dr., x-xi
   Interviewed the people of South Africa from Pretoria to Limpopo, the Free State to Kwazulu Natal, 11

   Africa must tell its story, 30

   More books should be written to create sufficient awareness to the history of decolonization of Africa, 30

Ogbu, Edwin Ogbe, 97

Olagunju, Dr. Tunji, vii

Olayiwola Abegunrin: 2009, 10, 36, 53

Olympic Games, 102

Onwobiko, K. B. C, 153

Orange Free State, 35

Oral transfer of knowledge, 153

Oral history is relegated to extinction, 153

Organization of African Unity (OAU)
Now transformed into the African Union (AU), 64, 70, 102, 106, 128

P

Palme, Olof, 90, 104-105

Pan African Congress (PAC), 23, 24, 44, 69, 89, 138

Pan Africanism,
Understanding the historical significance of, 9, 129

Phyllis Johnson and David Martins (1987), 115

Pierre du Toit, 27

"Pigeons"
Nigeria recruited "Pigeons" to send and receive correspondence from South Africa, 92, 101

Population Registration Act (1950), 16

R

Ransome-Kuti, Funmilayo, 77

Resentment in Post-Apartheid South Africa, 131

Riebeeck, Jan Van,
The European character that they claim founded South Africa, 36

Robben Island, 116

S

Salie, Ebrahim (2012), 38

Sankara, Thomas, 30, 77, 107

Security Council, 96

Seidler, Victor and Lawrence Blum (1989), 31

Seme, Pixley Ka Isaka, 52, 53
Founder of the African National Congress, 14

Senegal, 152

Separate Amenities Act, 46

Sharpeville Massacre of March 1960, ix, 24, 101

Shinkaiye, JK, 2002:12, 128

Sisulu, Walter, 53

Sobukwe, Robert of Pan African Congress, 14, 44, 78

South Africa
Nigeria's contributions to the Liberation struggle in South Africa, 123

Apartheid Regime, part of the ugly past of colonialism in Africa, ix

Oppressive administration of the white supremacist in South Africa, ix

African National Congress, ix, 14, 21, 69

South African freedom fighters were provided with Nigerian International passports, x

Many South African students were given scholarship by the Nigerian Government to study in Nigerian higher Institutions, x

Inappropriate documentation of the role of Nigeria in the liberation struggle, xi

Expulsion of apartheid South Africa from the commonwealth in 1961, xi

South African youths unaware of the Pan African spirit that pioneered the liberation struggle, xii

The role of Nigerian diplomacy at all levels in the collective fight for the liberation of South African, xii

Economic capabilities of South Africa, xii

Dlamini, known activist and a Local Champion of Post-Apartheid South African, 5

"Born free" South African Youths, 6, 8

Lack of understanding of the historical significance of Pan Africanism, 9

Teaching history in schools lack of emphasis, 9

Nigeria's leading role in dismantling apartheid in South Africa, 11

Many native South Africans aren't aware of the contribution of Nigeria or other "friends of freedom" against apartheid South Africa, 12

South Africa was the last country in Africa to gain political freedom or independence in 1994, 12, 14

Impact of the policy of segregation in South Africa, 16

Soweto uprising (1976), 16, 83

Enjoying the benevolence and spirit of Ubuntu from other Africans, 18

South African media, after 1994 was dominated by white supremacist and their cohorts, 22

Ideological differences between Nigeria and South Africa, 22

The liberation struggle still persist in a different dimension, 29

Union of South African (1910), 35

South African Republic (the Transvaal) and the Orange Free State (1850s), 35

Cape Colony and Natal, 35

Initiation of apartheid in South Africa in 1948 by its Chief architect Hendrik Verwoerd, 39

The hypocrisy of the United States and United Kingdom, 43

Boers now known officially as the Afrikaners, 38

South African Republic, 35, 48

South Africa, a nation in distress, 51

Exiled South Africans kept the flame of the liberation struggle burning, 56

Oil embargo by oil producing States placed on South Africa, 96

Freedom Park, a national monument, 124

Building a rich curriculum on history education is ripe, 150

Policy of silence about Nigeria contributions towards ending apartheid, 165

Young South Africans should be enlightened of an important part of the history of their struggle, 18

South African National Congress now African National Congress, ix, 14, 21, 69

South African Communist Party (SACP), 24, 84, 89, 108, 138

South African Media dominated by white supremacist and their cohorts, 22

Southern African Relief Fund (SARF), 120, 158, 159

Soviet Union, 72, 81, 83

Soweto uprising (1976), 16, 83

Steven Clark, 1993:9, 15

Sule, Maitama, 97, 114

Supreme Military Council, 120
  Made contributions to the Southern Africa Relief Fund (SAFR), 120

Sweden,
  Supported the liberation struggle in South Africa, 67, 90, 104

T

Tambo, Oliver R., 14, 53, 55, 56, 111,118

Tanzania,
  Contributors to the liberation struggle in South Africa, 4, 21, 137

Thabo Mbeki African School of Public and International Affairs, University of South African, vii

Thatcher, Margaret,
British Prime Minister visit to Nigeria, 1987, 63, 86

Toure, Ahmed Sekou, 77

Trade Union Congress of Nigeria, 63

Transferring history to individual, national and regional consciousness, 154

Tshope, Mark
Representative of Congress of South African Trade Union (COSATU) in Nigeria, 62

Tutu, Desmond (1994), 35, 53

U

Ubuntu, 11
Enjoying the benevolence and spirit of Ubuntu from other Africans, 18

Ubuntu is fixated on the concept of humanity, 18

Tale of African humanism and the project of the African character, 18

Ubuntu can be applied to governance, entertainment, science and technology, law etc, 19

Ubuntu is the African version of being your brother's keeper, 19

Reverse Ubuntu, 145

Uhomoibhi, Dr. Martin, vii

Umkhonto we Sizwe (MK) the youth wing of the National Congress, 53

Union Jack Flag burnt, 63

Union of South Africa, 35, 48

United Kingdom,
Margret Thatcher's visit to Nigeria, 1987, 63, 86

UK and US made the liberation struggle look like an ideological East versus West issue, 71

United Nations Declaration of Human Rights (UNDHR) 1948, 39

United Nations General Assembly (UNGA), 103

United Nations Resolution 421, 105

United Nations Special Committee Against Apartheid (UNSCA), 64, 71, 106

Nigeria headed this committee for 30 years, 99

United States,
Made the liberation struggle looked like an ideological East versus West issue, 71

University of South Africa vii,

V

Velthuizen, Prof. Andreas, vii

Verwored, Hendrik
Chief architect of Apartheid, 39

Vortrekker (the Great Trek), 37-38, 49

W

Wade, Abdulahi, 151

Worger, William and Nancy Clark (2022), 46

X

Xenophobia
After the collapse of apartheid resultant xenophobia that greeted the Africans as well as Nigerian Migrant, xi

Papers on xenophobia, 4

Quandary of self-hate and disdain for foreigners, 29

Love-hate relationship, 122

Y

Youth Solidarity for Southern African (YUSSA), 62

Z

Zambia,
Contributors to the liberation struggle in South Africa, 21, 88, 136

Zanawi, Meles, 151

Zimbabwe, 51, 59, 88, 92, 93, 109, 124, 168

Zinjiva Nkondo, 159
His former name was Victor Matlou, 159